# A CHAP'S GOT A CODE

# A CHAP'S GOT A CODE

TONY SALISBURY

**LIVE WIRE**

First published in 2005 by

Live Wire Books
The Orchard, School Lane
Warmington, Banbury
Oxfordshire OX17 1DE

Tel: 01295 690358
info@livewirebooks.com
www.livewirebooks.com

The right of Tony Salisbury to be identified as the
author of this work has been asserted in accordance
with the Copyright, Designs and Patents Act 1988.

ISBN 0-9542860-6-5

A catalogue record for this book is available from the
British Library.

Designed by Dick Malt
Printed and bound in Dubai
by Oriental Press

# CONTENTS

## SALISBURY'S XI

I   'Drybobs' and Pukka Chukkas      9
      (A Chap Learns the Code)

II   Marching Orders      23

III   Deb's Delight      39

IV   Down – and Out – In the Rockies      55

V   Halcyon Days      67

VI   TV Times      85

VII   All At Sea      101

VIII   Stars, Bars and Sticky Wickets      111

IX   A Capital Adventure      129

X   Golden Oldies      149

XI   A Good Innings      167

Index      179

For Jill

# ACKNOWLEDGEMENTS

I would first like to thank Michael Cable, of Live Wire Books, who helped me to produce joined-up writing, to create words of more than two syllables and to 'link' various incidents of my life.

I am also indebted to several very great friends who have seen me through all this with the assistance of a whisky or three. They are: Jan Barnes, Arthur Brittenden, Tony Darrell-Brown, Graham Dowson and his wife Denise, Charles Dudley, John Fox, Ron Miller and his wife Maureen, Adrian Tracey, Tim and Johnny Sergeant, Edward Priday, Raymond Kyle and Valerio, the inimitable maitre d' of Scalini Restaurant.

In addition, I appreciate enormously the interest and encouragement given to me by so many close friends at London Weekend Television, the Lord's Taverners and Capital Radio and especially by my two wonderful sisters, Jonet and Amanda, and my niece, Tatiana.

My special thanks to Sir Tim Rice for his very flattering comments – all lies (his words, not mine!) but still much appreciated.

And finally, but by no means least, Liza Myers, my friend and PA at Capital Radio in the early days of its life in 1973, who has put this whole tome into a computer from start to finish. Her patience, encouragement and correction of my spelling and punctuation are tremendously appreciated.

I should also add that I am unable to vouch completely for the accuracy of some of the dates included, as the contents of this book are the outpourings of an addled mind, with no diaries to refer to.

I wish I could have included mentions of all the many friends and colleagues with whom I have worked and played over the years at

Southern Television, LWT and Capital, but that would have meant running to two volumes! To each and every one of you, I raise my glass with a heartfelt: "Thanks for everything."

# I

## 'DRYBOBS' AND PUKKA CHUKKAS

I WAS BORN IN 1927. This happens to have been a vintage year for cricket during which Don Bradman made his first-class debut in Australia and the great Wally Hammond played his maiden Test for England. As a lifelong cricket fanatic, I do rather regret the fact that my own arrival at the crease of life in that same year turned out to be a somewhat less significant landmark in the annals of cricketing history! Even to my parents, the event of my birth seems to have provided little more than a temporary distraction.

My mother was tall, slim, direct and very imposing. She was always immaculately dressed by Chanel and, in her later years, was accompanied everywhere she went by two jewellery cases. The larger of these she filled with bottles of gin, the other with tonic. She loved to wear chunky jewellery and had a very large assortment of sunglasses that she had collected on her regular visits to Nice, Cannes, Monaco and some of the other more stylish and fashionable resorts of Europe.

Her name was Muriel, but she was known to her friends as Mickey, which she much preferred. The only child of a very wealthy and successful businessman, Sir Archie Mitchelson, she was spoiled rotten by her doting and indulgent father. She never went to school, but was educated at home by a governess before immersing herself, at the earliest opportunity, in the fashionable London social scene of the time. At The 400, her favourite nightclub in Leicester Square, she became renowned for her uninhibited dancing of the Charleston. Another of her regular haunts was the Café de Paris, where, some years later, she narrowly survived the wartime bombing raid that killed three people sitting at a nearby table.

Sadly, I never knew my father. Jack Salisbury was twenty-one and my mother just twenty when they married. I arrived ten months later. The following year they were divorced and there was no further contact between father and son. This was a pity because, from what I can gather, he and I would have got on famously. He was a great sportsman, who went on to ski for England in the 1930's and was also a leading Cresta Run competitor. Tragically, he then lost a leg as a result of a skiing accident and, totally unable to come to terms with this crippling setback, fell into a deep depression and took to the bottle, which contributed to his death at the age of only thirty-nine.

I didn't get to know any of this until much later, because my mother remarried when I was three years old and I grew up believing that the second of her three husbands – cavalry officer and polo player Alex Barclay – was my natural father. I was fifteen or sixteen before I discovered the truth.

My stepfather remained a rather remote figure. Quite apart from the physical and emotional distance that was carefully maintained between us in the accepted stiff-upper-lip manner of the times, I never got on too well with him. When I think back, I can't remember him ever smiling.

As one of the top polo players in the country, he represented England several times during the early thirties and also ran his own private team. This featured regular guest appearances by visiting players from Argentina and the USA, including quite a few Hollywood stars, many of whom stayed at our home, Edmundsbury, a grand Tudor house near New Malden, just off what is now the Kingston by-pass.

The property, which included stables for six polo ponies, was actually owned by my grandfather. Sir Archie, who was said to have bought his title for £5,000 during Lloyd George's premiership, had amassed a very sizeable fortune from mining interests in the North East and some very shrewd investments. He was also one of the founders of Great Universal Stores and, as chairman, was responsible for bringing in the great Isaac Woolfson, who famously went on to build GUS into one of the biggest and most successful companies in the country. Grandpa helped to pay for just about everything, his wealth enabling my parents to keep up appearances even during the worst depression years of the thirties.

My mother had two children by Alex Barclay, my half-sisters Jonet and Amanda. Jonet should actually have been 'Janet', but 'Jonet' was entered on her birth certificate by mistake and my mother then decided that she rather liked the sound of it. So, Jonet it was.

All three of us were looked after by a nanny, Bubba, and packed off to boarding school at the earliest opportunity, as was the fashion at the time, so that our parents could enjoy their hectic social life without respite.

In many ways, Bubba was much more of a mum to me than my mother ever was. Like all the wonderful nannies of that era, she was a spinster and all the love she had to give was reserved for her charges, whom she regarded as her own children. From the time I was first sent off to boarding school at the age of five, I would normally only see my mother once during the course of each term. At home, I would generally be brought down between 6.00 and 6.30 in the evening to spend half-an-hour with her before she embarked on her social rounds. The rest of the time was spent with Bubba and the other servants, of whom there were several in the house, including a cook called Bassey.

Bassey and Bubba gave every appearance of disliking each other intensely. In particular, they were fiercely protective of their own territory, the kitchen and the nursery respectively, my mother being called in to arbitrate over any disputed border incursions. This went on for years and arose out of below stairs snobbery, Bubba and Bassey each being convinced that their position was superior to that of the other. However, it was obviously a love/hate relationship because when Bassey died she left all her money to Bubba.

Throughout the 1930s Edmundsbury was a whirl of social activity – dances, cocktail parties, weekend house parties, tennis parties, polo matches and even bicycle polo! And among the celebrities who either stayed or visited at this time were Lord and Lady Mountbatten, the Duke and Duchess of Gloucester, Leslie Howard, Douglas Fairbanks Jnr and the formidable Tallulah Bankhead.

I remember Tallulah Bankhead especially well because of an incident involving Jonet, the elder of my two half-sisters. Nanny Bubba had been ordered to go and find Jonet, then about five years old, and bring her to the drawing room to be introduced to Miss Bankhead. As Bubba duly ushered her in, my mother announced: "Tallulah, I would like you to meet my daughter, Jonet."

Tallulah, drawing on a cigarette encased in an enormously long, elegant holder, gazed down at this angelic-looking child and drawled: "Well – hello, Honey."

To which Jonet immediately responded – quite reasonably I thought – with: "Hello, Marmalade." Whereupon she was immediately taken out for a sound spanking.

I, too, had my moments.

Cruises were very fashionable at this time and it was on one of the rare occasions when my parents took me along with them that I became drunk for the first time and nearly found myself accused of rape as a result – at the age of five!

My mother had come to my cabin straight from a cocktail party to settle me down for the night before going on to dinner. She had a powerful Martini in her hand, which she put down while she kissed me goodnight and then promptly forgot about. I woke up later wanting a drink of water and gulped down the Martini. Not long afterwards a very large Dutch lady in the adjoining cabin was heard to scream for help as a young, inebriated child tried to climb into the bunk with her.

On a couple of occasions, when Bubba was on holiday, temporary nannies were hired to look after me. Both lasted only a week, the first quite understandably deciding to call it a day prematurely after I tried to murder her. She was a large, red-haired woman to whom I took an immediate and immense dislike. We were at the seaside at Frinton one day and she was paddling, with her back to the beach. Relaxing with a large gin-and-tonic under a sunshade some distance away, my mother looked on, completely unconcerned, as her beloved little five-year-old picked up his junior cricket bat and started creeping towards the unsuspecting nanny. Mother still thought it was just a bit of a game when I started to attack the unfortunate woman with my bat. In fact, I walloped her over the head so hard that she needed several stitches. The next day she was gone.

The second temporary nanny's departure was definitely not my fault.

Lord Louis Mountbatten and his wife, Edwina, were visiting Edmundsbury – and at that time Edwina had taken to travelling everywhere with a not quite fully-grown lion that she had somehow acquired as a pet! Knowing nothing of this in advance, the nanny walked into the nursery to find me wrestling on the floor with the lion. She left the house in hysterics.

Growing up in this environment was often quite exciting, but could also sometimes be overwhelming. Both mother and Alex tended to be somewhat intolerant of my shortcomings and, as a result, I became rather shy and awkward in the company of grown-ups, with occasionally mortifying consequences.

There was, for instance, the time when I was coached at great length on exactly how to bow when introduced to the Duchess of Gloucester, who happened to be visiting the house. When the moment came, I did all the right things, forgetting only that I had a large glass of orange juice clutched in my hand. As I executed my perfect bow, this tipped all over the Duchess's dress.

Almost equally embarrassing was the occasion at a cocktail party when I was introduced to a guest who, I had been warned in advance, was liable to come out with a few loud and outrageous remarks. He asked me where I went to school and when I told him I was at Eton he shouted: "Ah! I was at Eton, too, but only for a short time. I was expelled."

"Oh, really," I said, not quite knowing how to react to this revelation.

There was a pause before he bellowed: "Don't you want to know why?"

"Well, yes, Sir, if you'd like to tell me," I replied nervously.

"Buggery, my dear boy, buggery!" he barked.

The first twelve years of my life are a jumble of such 'Upstairs, Downstairs' memories. Then came September 3rd, 1939. We were staying at Chirk Castle in North Wales, as guests of Lord and Lady Howard de Walden, when, over the radio, came the announcement from Neville Chamberlain that was to change all our lives for ever. I think it is fair to say that at that precise moment an era ended.

While my stepfather went off to war with his regiment, the Queen's Bays (2nd Dragoon Guards) – soon to join the ill-fated British Expeditionary Force in France – I went up to Eton.

Eton is divided into twenty-five Houses, each with around forty boys, but, unlike almost every other public school in the country, it has never had dormitories. Instead, each boy has his own tiny bedroom/study from the day he first arrives there. So, right from the start, you are very much on your own. The fact that I had already been boarding at prep school since I was five meant that I was better prepared than most to cope with the routine and I didn't really suffer at all from homesickness. Even so, I didn't enjoy it very much.

My time there coincided almost exactly with the six years of the war. One side effect of this was that the staff tended to be rather elderly, all the younger masters having been called up. There was also a lot of bullying, as well as occasional thrashings administered by the members of The Library – the Head of School, the Captain of Games and various other senior boys in each House. Looking back, this was absolutely dreadful, pure sadism in my view. Fagging, on the other hand, was not a problem – in fact, I thought it was quite fun. Again, it was the members of The Library who had the right to shout "Boy!" – whereupon every fag within earshot had to drop whatever he was doing and race to answer the call, the last one to arrive having to do whatever menial chore was required.

Lessons started before breakfast, with the first class at 7.30am, but every other afternoon was set aside for sport. There was no set prep. You were left to look after yourself in that respect. For instance, your history master might instruct you to produce an essay on King John in three weeks time and it was then up to you to decide when you did it, fitting it in when you could amongst your various other commitments. The very admirable idea, of course, was to encourage independence and self-discipline.

A lot of emphasis was laid on sport – the playing fields of Eton and all that! This suited me fine because I enjoyed my sport and certainly showed more aptitude for it than I ever did for any academic endeavour. I played squash and fives and also the Eton Field Game –

a mixture of rugby and soccer, not to be confused with the Eton Wall Game, which was something quite different. But it was cricket that I loved best of all, rather appropriately given that one of my Godfathers was Douglas Jardine, the captain of England during the notorious 'bodyline' series in Australia. In the summer term you were either a 'drybob' (cricketer) or a 'wetbob' (rower). If you hated the idea of both you were required to go for long-distance runs instead. As a reasonable top order batsman and a very energetic fielder in the covers, I played regularly in the school teams although, sadly, I never quite made it to Lord's with the 1st XI for the annual Eton v. Harrow match.

Lord's is where the match has always traditionally been staged, but it was not available during the war years, so the two teams met either at Eton or Harrow. Although, years later, I did get to play in a charity match at the Oval on one occasion, I never had another opportunity to live out every weekend cricketer's fantasy of playing at Lords, walking through the Long Room, down the steps and out to bat on the square at cricket's historic headquarters. That remains one of the great disappointments of my life.

A more amusing highlight of my schoolboy cricketing career took place during the summer holiday of 1943, when I was about sixteen, and involved a match at a friend's stately home.

I had several aristocratic friends at Eton, although at that age one tended to be unimpressed by that sort of thing. For instance, one of my best pals, known to one and all simply as Percy Minor, was, in fact, the younger son of the Duke of Northumberland, while his older brother, the heir to the Dukedom, was Percy Major. Also in my class was a very nice young chap called Hugh, who just happened to be second in line to another of the most famous earldoms in the country, with not just one family seat to its name, but two! The second of these was just outside Reading and consisted of a 30,000-acre estate and a huge house with more than forty bedrooms. I don't want to identify the family more precisely for reasons that will become clear from what follows.

Hugh had invited me down to their Berkshire place for the weekend in order to play cricket for his mother's XI against the estate workers. Clutching a brown paper carrier bag containing my cricket flannels, shirt and boots, still dirty from the previous outing, I duly arrived by train at Reading station, where Hugh had told me someone would be waiting to pick me up and take me on to the house. What he hadn't made quite clear was that I was to be met by a chauffeur-driven Rolls Royce!

After turning off the road and onto a seemingly endless drive that wound through lush parkland, we eventually arrived at the house and I found myself getting out of the Rolls at the foot of a curved flight of twenty wide stone steps leading up to a very grand front entrance. Three footmen were in position on the steps and a butler was standing at the top in regal splendour, waiting to receive me.

Much to my embarrassment, the chauffeur insisted on taking my carrier bag, which he then handed to a footman, who passed it up to the next footman, who passed it on to the next, who in turn gave it to the butler. He held it at arm's length, with a look of slight distaste on his face, as though he were carrying a parcel of rotting fish.

Inside the house, I was led up a series of staircases and along a maze of corridors to my room. Here, the butler rather pointedly suggested that I might like to take a bath, adding that he would arrange to have my cricket gear pressed. Perhaps I would then care to come down to join master Hugh and the other members of the team, he added.

I had my bath and returned to the room to find my gear laid out on the bed, still filthy, but perfectly pressed. I hurriedly changed into it and spent the next fifteen minutes trying to find my way downstairs. I eventually stumbled into an enormous, elegant and beautifully furnished drawing room with a vast ornate fireplace at one end in which a log fire was blazing away, despite the fact that it was a warm June day. Seated on the wooden fire surround, with a large gin-and-tonic cradled in her hands, was a very aristocratic looking lady who I realised instantly must be Hugh's mother. I advanced, hand outstretched, and got as far as saying: "Good morning, your Ladyship", when, to my horror, she lurched rather unsteadily to her feet and toppled backwards into the fire.

I rushed forward and pulled her out, beating at burning bits of her clothing, and was about to shout for help when she asked very calmly, but with her words slightly slurred: "What have you done with my drink, young man?"

At this point a housekeeper rushed in and gently led her away as some of the other guest players started to arrive. To my amazement, she returned half-an-hour later, apparently none the worse for wear, to host the buffet lunch that had been laid on before the match, behaving as if nothing untoward had happened.

As we prepared for the game, she then announced to her team that anyone hitting the ball for six into the pond at one end of the ground would receive ten shillings, a considerable amount of money in 1943.

It was a beautiful afternoon as the opposition took to the field, my team having been put in to bat first. A wicket fell and I was next man in. As I walked to the crease, the opposition captain sidled up to me and asked: "Do I understand, sir, that her Ladyship has offered ten shillings for every six hit into the pond?"

"Quite correct," I replied brightly.

"Well, sir, it occurred to me that we might come to some reasonable arrangement, if you get my meaning."

"Say no more – how about 50/50?" I suggested.

"You're on!" he said, beaming. He immediately put himself on to bowl and proceeded to send down a series of six long hops, no less than four of which I managed to despatch into the water. Four more followed in his next over before he decided it was time to call a halt and started bowling a better length. Later, we shared our winnings behind the pavilion – two quid each!

That evening there was a formal dinner party for sixteen in the great dining room. In spite of the fact that the war was raging and rationing was supposed to be in force, we were served five courses, with six bewigged footmen standing behind us. Unbelievable!

I found myself seated next to Her Ladyship, who, as I had realised by this time, was almost permanently inebriated. At one point during the meal she leaned across to me and slurred: "You know, I hate this bloody war – you just can't get any servants."

As conversation stopper go, that's pretty hard to beat, although many years later I did hear an even more terminal one from holiday camp tycoon Fred Pontin. It came during a Lord's Taverners dinner at the Café Royal. I was sitting next to Fred and although I hadn't had the pleasure of meeting him before I happened to know that both he and his great rival, Sir Billy Butlin, had known my grand-father and this enabled me to break the ice. Not that the ice needed to be broken with Fred as he was enormously gregarious and a great raconteur.

For some reason, as the first course was being served, he began to talk with great humour about his various medical problems. In fact, he got quite carried away, mainly, I suspect, because I was, as ever, a polite listener and made the odd sympathetic noise. He soon got on to the most serious of his problems about which he appeared very proud, namely his need to make use of a colostomy bag or "second stomach" as he referred to it. "Just like the Queen Mum's," he added, as if this somehow put him on a par with her.

By now, the main course was being served and at the very moment that he was elaborating on the advantages of having a colostomy bag, the waitress leaned over his shoulder and placed a large, juicy steak before him. Fred picked up his knife and fork and turning to me as my steak was placed in front of me, said casually: "As a matter of fact, I'm having a shit right now."

Back at Eton, we were not always quite so effectively insulated from the harsher realities of the war as Her Ladyship and her bewigged servants. Whether it was because we just happened to be under the flight path of bombers jettisoning their remaining payload after raids on London or, more likely, because of our proximity to Windsor Castle, we occasionally found ourselves in the firing line. One night, a 1000lb landed in Chapel Yard, just outside my House, blowing in all the windows. Fortunately, my curtains were drawn at the time.

Later, a second bomb landed in School Yard but failed to explode. As a bomb disposal team arrived to dismantle it, we were all evacuated to a safe distance. All of us, that is, except Lord Hugh Cecil, then the Provost of Eton College. As members of the disposal unit were very cautiously examining the bomb inch by inch, the very elderly and rather absent-minded Lord Cecil suddenly came shuffling into School Yard and peered down into the crater. Before the horrified experts could stop him, he then prodded the outer casing of the device vigorously with the end of his walking stick, demanding: "Well, what's the matter with the bloody thing?"

Later, came the flying bombs – the doodlebugs. We quickly learned to recognise their distinctive sound as they came overhead, and if the sound suddenly cut out you took whatever cover was available.

It was during this particular period that I had to sit my school certificate, the precursor of GCSEs and A Levels. It used to be the rule at Eton that each House Master had a maximum tenure of fourteen years and it just happened that this was my House Master's final year. He had never had a boy fail the School Certificate and he was determined to keep his 100% success rate. However, he was anxious that I was going to let him down – and with good reason. I had, after all, entered Eton at the very bottom of the lowest entry class and had shown no great signs of improvement.

We sat the exams over a number of days and throughout this time the flying bombs were coming over. Every time one cut out, we would dive for cover under our desks until the danger cleared. None of this was very frightening to us. On the contrary, as sixteen and seventeen-years-olds we found it rather exciting. However, the examiners, realising that we had had to work under the most unusual circumstances and that these bombing raids might possibly have had an unsettling effect on certain boys, wrote to the school suggesting that if they knew of any particular cases where this was true then they should name those individuals so that this could be taken into account in assessing their results.

My long-suffering House Master, who was also my Tutor, grasped this opportunity with both hands and informed them that he had one boy whose nerves had been so badly affected by these blasted flying bombs that he had become nothing short of a blithering idiot. The authorities accepted his word and I duly received the coveted School Certificate. My only regret was that, amid much jollity, he then felt it necessary to recount the story to the entire House at my leaving dinner. Until that moment, I had been feeling very pleased with myself for having done it all on my own.

As it happens, I could have got my own back and raised a few laughs at his expense had I chosen to reveal the truth about his clumsy attempts at sex education. This was apparently considered to be part of a House Master's duty towards his charges, but I suspect they all found it an awkward subject to broach in those less enlightened days.

I was fourteen years old when he came into my room one evening just after lights out and, after a considerable amount of coughing and spluttering in the darkness, blurted out: "Tell me, Salisbury, do you ever...ever...ever have funny feelings...er...between your legs? (Cough! Cough!)

Realising immediately what he might be driving at and anxious to help him out of his embarrassment, I replied: "Well, yes, sir – occasionally."

This was greeted with a tremendous amount of nervous coughing and spluttering at the end of which he muttered: "Well, put a cold sponge on it, my boy. Goodnight."

As it happens, my sexual awakening didn't actual happen until about three years later when I was seventeen. We all tended to be late starters in those days!

I was leaning out of my top floor window in B.G. Whitfield's House at about five o'clock one evening when I noticed this beautiful, long-haired brunette cycling past in the street down below, with skirts flying. She appeared again at the same time the next day, and the next....

I became quite besotted and made a point of being on watch at my window every evening. I decided she must be biking to and from work each day, possibly in Slough. Then, after a couple of weeks, Eureka! She happened to look up, caught my eye – and smiled and waved. I was no longer besotted; I was in love. But what could I do? How could I make contact? It was an impossible situation.

I had to wait until the next school holiday to find a solution. By this time, for reasons that will be explained later, my mother and my sisters had moved from Edmundsbury to a house on the river in Old Windsor, just five miles down the road from Eton. A historic house, known as The White Hermitage, the place had originally been built by Henry VIII for Anne Boleyn.

On the first day of the holidays, I made some elaborate excuse, got on my bike and cycled back to school, taking up position outside my House at 8.30am, when I reckoned that the object of my adolescent desires might be making the outward journey to work. I had never been able to check this before because I would be in class at that time of the morning.

Sure enough, she came flashing past about half-an-hour after I had taken up position. I followed at a discreet distance and discovered that, just as I had suspected, she was indeed bound for Slough, where she eventually disappeared into a small factory. That evening, having whiled away most of the day in a local cinema, I returned to the factory gate at 4.00pm and waited for her to re-emerge. When she duly appeared and rode off I again followed her, a bit closer this time. I still couldn't quite pluck up the courage to pull alongside, although it was obvious that she knew I was there.

Eventually, just as we got back to Eton High Street, I made my move. I drew alongside, took a deep breath and blurted out: "My-name's-Tony-will-you-come-to-the-cinema-with-me-tonight?"

"I'd love to," she replied, flashing a smile that almost knocked me right off my bike. "See you at the Ritz at seven."

I rode back to Old Windsor in a state of high excitement, had a bath, changed, borrowed £5 from my mother and arrived breathlessly at the Ritz an hour early. My 'date' arrived promptly at seven o'clock, looking stunning.

I purchased two 3/6d seats in the stalls and, having heard all about the sort of activities that could be enjoyed in relative privacy of the back row, headed in that direction. Perfect. Two cosy seats and the prospect of three hours in the semi-darkness with the prettiest girl in the world – what more could a young man ask for?

A friend had told me that Plan A should involve first holding hands before making any further move. So fraction-by-fraction, my hand inched towards hers. Two hours and fifty minutes later, our fingers touched. The thrill was incredible.

I would like to be able to say that this beautiful English rose took my hand and then melted into my arms, instead of which what she actually did was to press 3/6d into my palm before jumping up with the words: "Ta for taking me to the flicks, I really wanted to see that film – but I must be off now." She made it abundantly clear that she wasn't in the least bit interested in me and that I would not be seeing her again. I was completely crestfallen and went off the opposite sex for at least a week.

They say that all is fair in love and war – and I was to get my first experience of both in very quick succession.

# II

## MARCHING ORDERS

I HAD NEVER REALLY GIVEN that much thought to what I wanted to do after I left school. It had always been assumed that I would follow my stepfather into the Army, where his position as Colonel of the Queen's Bays virtually guaranteed a commission. If that didn't work out for any reason, I would probably end up as something in the City. As it turned out, I didn't have any choice in the matter initially because the war was still on when I left Eton in December 1944 and, like most of my contemporaries, I immediately enlisted.

Boarding school was the perfect preparation for the rigours of Army life. When, like me, you had been living away from home at various schools since the age of five, it came as no great shock to the system to find yourself in a barrack room. You weren't as homesick as many others and you didn't want to fly back to mum. It was quite normal to be on your own and you had long ago learned to be independent and to look after yourself. In that respect, Old Etonians were often able to cope with the situation much better than tough working class kids who had never before been separated from their families.

Even so, I was nervous with anticipation as I boarded a train at Waterloo, bound for Bovingdon camp in Dorset and eight weeks of basic training before going on to do a four-month Officer Cadet Training Course. The train was packed with young men all bound for the same destination and, as so often happens in that sort of situation, the first person I got talking to in the crowded corridor became my best mate for the duration. His name was Searle. A trainee London bus driver, he was a very savvy sort of chap, a bit older than me. Far from being hostile when he found out that I was fresh out of Eton, he immediately volunteered to take me under his wing and show me the ropes, assuming, quite rightly, that I would be pretty useless at things like pressing my uniform.

Even with Searle to keep an eye out for me, those eight weeks at Bovingdon were pretty uncomfortable. The January of 1945 was one of the coldest on record, and in the unheated barrack room, where each of us was allowed only one thin blanket, the nights were freezing, so much so that it was almost a relief when Reveille was sounded at 6.00am and you could get up and start moving around. By 6.30 you were out on the parade ground, breakfast was at 7.30 and by eight o'clock you were back for more square-bashing.

We were relatively lucky because although our Sgt Major was a bastard, he was a bastard in the nicest possible way. "Am I 'urting you, Salisbury? ", he would bellow in your ear, standing so close behind you that you could feel his hot breath on your neck. "No? Well, I should be – because I'm standing on your f****** hair!" That was about as bad as it got with him and the hardest thing about it was trying to keep a straight face. But some of the others could be really sadistic. For instance, you had to fold your kit up just right and sometimes they'd chuck the whole lot out of the window and into the slush for no real reason. Or they would jump on the barrack room table and march up and down on it in their muddy boots before screaming: "This table's filthy – you've got ten minutes to clean it." The whole idea, of course, was to teach you how to take orders, but you didn't realise this at the time and some of these Sergeants became hate figures.

When I moved on to the Officer Cadet Training Unit, I did actually come into contact with the most famous Regimental Sergeant Major of them all – RSM Brittain. It was claimed that on a still morning his surprisingly high-pitched voice could be a mile away as he screeched orders on the parade ground. And I can personally vouch for the fact that his eyesight was so keen that he could spot an undone tunic button on a cadet three rows back in a parade of two hundred men.

He did, however, have a twisted sense of humour. Among my intake was King Hussein of Jordan. I was some distance away as Brittain went down the line of cadets one morning during inspection and stopped in front of the king, who, at just five-foot-five, was dwarfed by the RSM's six-foot-two. Brittain looked him up and down for a moment and then, spotting something very slightly awry with his dress, drew himself up to his full height and bellowed: "You're an 'orrible little king! Sir!!"

Also in my squad was Jeremy Ash, who went on much later to become a famous and successful racehorse owner. At seventeen, Jeremy owned more land and was probably richer than anyone in the unit, including most of the officers. He somehow managed to run a Rolls Royce, which, rather cheekily, he would park next to the Commanding Officer's jeep. How and from where he managed to get hold of the petrol for it at a time when strict rationing was in force was a matter of considerable conjecture in the Mess.

Right from the start, it was clear that he would never make a soldier of any rank. In that respect, he was completely and utterly useless. Apart from anything else, he was a large, bumbling and rather untidy figure, with very little dress sense and absolutely no co-ordination. He was, however, a very nice, kind person whose popularity among his 'brothers in arms' was such that we did all we possibly could to protect him from the wrath of Brittain and all the other fearsome sergeants.

Aside from the total lack of co-ordination that made it almost impossible for him to march in step, he also had an unhappy knack of forgetting odd items of kit and clothing when going on parade. This failing was most memorably demonstrated on the day that all Officer Cadets were on the Adjutant's parade. Before assembling, we carefully double-checked Jeremy's clothing from head to foot, making sure that his buttons were all done up, his beret on at the right angle and so on. It was only when the RSM called us to attention and then ordered us to stand at ease, immediately prior to inspection, that I glanced across and realised to my horror that we had all forgotten one vital thing.

Jeremy, for once, was looking immaculate as he stood there, perfectly correct, in the 'at ease' position – shoulders back, chin up and feet exactly the right distance apart, his outstretched right arm holding his rifle at exactly the right angle. Except there was no rifle!

Now, it is often true that something as obvious as a missing rifle goes unnoticed, while a slightly tarnished or undone tunic button will be spotted from the other side of the parade ground. This was very nearly the case on this occasion. The Colonel moved down the line, past me and past Jeremy, looking each one of us up and down without batting an eyelid. So did the Second-In-Command. The Adjutant also passed by and was three cadets further down the line before he did a sudden double take, spun on his heel and darted back, colliding with the RSM as he did so. Both stared at Jeremy in disbelief.

"Take that man's name," barked the Adjutant, marching on down the line.

"What's your name, Ash?" screamed the RSM.

"Ash, Sir," said Jeremy, in a tone of voice that implied all this was a fuss about nothing.

There was a moment's pause and then, with a sinister, knowing smirk playing about his lips, the RSM pushed his face to within an inch of Jeremy's ear and said very quietly: "How much petrol have you got, Ash?"

Jeremy got the message right away – and duly survived to live and train another day.

I was still barely eighteen at this time and very naïve and innocent. Among other things, I had certainly not yet learned how to hold my liquor, as I discovered to my cost when, along with squad mate Norman Lonsdale, I ventured out on my first pub-crawl in Aldershot.

In order to enliven the proceedings while at the same time saving some money, our plan was to order glasses of orange juice and then surreptitiously top them up with whisky, a bottle of which I had managed to pinch from my mother's well-stocked drinks cabinet at home. Unfortunately, this plan had to be abandoned when we arrived in Aldershot to find that all the pubs had been temporarily closed due to rioting by Canadian soldiers, a not uncommon occurrence, we were told. We decided instead to go to the cinema, where we fortified ourselves throughout the film with swigs of neat whisky from the bottle. I had never drunk whisky before, which probably explains a lot of what was to follow.

The film was entitled '29 Acacia Avenue' and starred Gordon Harker. For some reason, that has always stuck in my mind. Norman and I settled ourselves in the middle of the third row of the stalls, where we sipped from the bottle at regular intervals until, about an hour into the film, I started to feel distinctly queasy. I decided to retire to the gents, which I managed to reach in reasonably good order before my head started swimming. I recall trying to steady myself against a pillar, only to find that I kept sliding none too gracefully to the floor. After a few minutes, I rather unwisely decided that I would return to my seat.

The gents' was located just to one side of the screen and, as I made my way unsteadily back, I managed to sit in the lap of virtually everyone in the front row. I thought I had spotted Norman in the middle of the third row, but somehow lost my bearings in the semi-darkness and entered the fifth row, causing even more disruption as I stumbled towards the middle. It was then that I realised that Norman was actually two rows further down. A couple were entwined immediately in front of me and I simply parted their heads and stepped over the seats between them, eventually plonking myself down next to Norman. He realised that the sensible thing would be to get me out of there as soon as possible, find a taxi and return to the barracks.

As we were weaving along the street in search of a cab, Norman then suddenly hissed in my ear: "For God's sake, stand up properly and try to walk straight – there are two Military Policemen approaching!" At that precise moment, I decided to have a little rest …in the gutter. Now, I am not suggesting that those MPs were bought off by Norman, but their interest in me did seem to be very effectively diverted by the large, white £5 note that he allowed to flutter onto the pavement.

A reluctant taxi driver was eventually found and, on condition that I kept my head stuck out of the window all the way, he agreed to drive us back to the barracks. Norman, still valiantly trying to protect my well-being despite himself being in a pretty befuddled state, managed to get me to my bunk and then started back to his own barrack room, which was on the other side of the square. Unfortunately, he only got halfway across the square before being overcome by fatigue. Even though it was freezing cold, with two inches of snow on the ground, he decided to sit down and rest for a moment. He was still there, fast asleep, at 6.00am the next morning when the RSM found him and immediately put him on a charge

I felt terribly guilty when I found out what had happened and longed for a chance to repay the favour. The opportunity never came. I lost track of Norman after we both moved on from the OCTU and I heard nothing much more about him until some years later when he enjoyed some brief moments of celebrity as a result of a close and much-publicised friendship with a member of the Royal Family.

The Officer Cadet Training Course involved six months extensive training in all aspects of soldiering and leadership. Amongst other things, you learned to drive tanks, three-tonners, Scammels and anything else that moved. You crossed fields on your belly, with live bullets whistling over your head, and you were required to pass various regular tests. If you failed, you were 'retarded', which meant that you were sent back for an extra month's training.

My greatest problems arose during the Driving and Maintenance section of the course. My driving was fine, but I was unable to understand all the bits and pieces under the bonnet. When asked during one test to point out and explain the workings of the sump, I walked to the back of the vehicle and hopefully opened the boot! I think I was saved from being retarded only due to the fact that by this time I had two stepfathers, both of them high-ranking officers in cavalry regiments.

It was during the very early part of the war that my mother divorced SF1 (Stepfather No. 1, Alex Barclay) and married SF2. This was a particularly complicated and messy business because while SF1 was the Colonel in charge of the Queen's Bays, SF2, Mark Roddick, was the Colonel in charge of the 10th Hussars, a sister regiment to the Queen's Bays. These sister regiments tended to be very close-knit, so everybody would have known about the scandalous progress of the affair and I can only imagine that this must have resulted in considerable emotional stress and immense embarrassment for both men, but particularly SF1.

This already delicate situation then became even more highly charged in 1941 when SF2 was promoted to Brigadier and put in command of the 2nd Armoured Brigade in North Africa, which included SF1's regiment. That clearly had the potential to be almost impossibly awkward. The two men did fight alongside each other at El Alamein, but shortly afterwards SF1 was posted to America to teach tank warfare, probably at his own request, I suspect. SF2 was later wounded in North Africa, losing a finger in a mine explosion that also left him with a piece of shrapnel lodged in his brain.

My own war record was rather undistinguished, since I just missed all the action. I was still in training at OCTU when the war in Europe ended. Then, having been commissioned as a Sub-Lieutenant in the Queen's Bays, I joined the regiment at Palmanova in Italy on VJ Day.

The nearest I ever got to a taste of 'combat' was a football match against the 'enemy'! I had been with the regiment in Italy for about three months when my squadron was posted to Yugoslavia in order to help keep the peace among rebel groups who were stirring up trouble against Tito. We were camped under canvas in a desolate mountain area, where I was immediately taken ill with some form of virus, serious enough for me to be rushed back to hospital in Trieste. Having returned to duty after a couple of weeks, I was immediately ordered to take part in a 'goodwill' soccer match that had been arranged against the rebels.

The 'pitch' was an uneven, stone-strewn and completely grassless area of open ground surrounded by mountains and forests. We prepared by picking up as many of the stones as possible and a couple of jeeps were then lined up at each end to serve as goalposts. We were in the process of discussing what to use for corner flags when the opposition arrived. Armed to the teeth, with rifles slung over their shoulders and bandoleers around their waists, they were the most unnerving group of men I had ever seen.

Everybody shook hands and then, with a flourish, we produced the football. All that we were still missing were corner flags. We tried to explain this, but language difficulties caused total confusion until we resorted to mime, a trooper being dispatched to each corner in turn, where he stood waving one arm. At this point the partisans seemed to get the message. With much smiling and nodding and gestures indicating that we should hang on a minute while they sorted the matter out, they disappeared over the hill whence they had come and returned triumphantly a few minutes later with four mounted and fully-loaded machine guns, which they proceeded to set up at each corner.

We couldn't help noticing as we took up our positions for the kick-off that not only were all four corner flags pointing inwards and, therefore, directly at us, but that there was a partisan sitting behind each one of them, thus sending out what appeared to us to be an unmistakable signal. Needless to say, we played a hard game and were unlucky to lose 16-0!

Back in Italy, our duties were generally a good deal less arduous and we regularly spent our weekends in Venice or Trieste. There was even a bit of drag hunting. If that all sounds a little incongruous, it is important to remember that the war had been won by this time and for those who had been involved in the especially bitter fighting of the Italian campaign there was every reason to be able to enjoy a bit of relaxation. For Johnny-Come-Latelys like me, relief at having so narrowly missed the worst horrors of the fighting was tinged with guilt that we were having things so easy.

My two closest friends in the regiment at this time were John Penney, who became a BBC racing commentator, and John Griffin, who went on to be the Queen Mother's ADC for about thirty years. In Venice, the Army had taken over the Danielli Hotel and as an officer you could have a room there for just five-shillings-a-night. We used to go to Harry's Bar, where I met Harry himself, and it was after a particularly good dinner there one evening that I staggered out into the 'street' to hail a taxi and, momentarily forgetting where I was, fell into the canal.

I'm pleased to say that I conducted myself with a little more decorum when, during my first spell of leave back in England a few weeks later, I got a taste of another legendary establishment, staying at the Cavendish Hotel in London. The hotel was originally presided over by Rosa Lewis, a former cook from a stately home who had caught the eye of the future Edward VII and became his mistress. When he became King, he bought her the Cavendish, which she ran with some style for the rest of her life. Under Rosa, it was a very high-class and yet distinctly racy establishment, where members of the Royal Family and the nobility could bring their chorus girls or whatever, secure in the knowledge that their activities would be treated with the utmost discretion. Apart from this being considered normal and quite acceptable behaviour among the ruling classes of the time, there were no tabloid papers and paparazzi around to spill the beans and spoil their fun.

During the Great War, Rosa then turned the hotel into a recuperation centre for officers from the Front, famously rising from her chair on the day that war was declared to remove a signed photo of the Kaiser from her drawing room wall and then solemnly hanging it in the lavatory instead. The whole story was told in the hugely successful television series The Duchess of Duke Street.

It was my mother who suggested that I should stay there while I was in London on leave, pointing out that my father had been something of a regular. I booked for a week and arrived in the foyer to find the odd polo stick lying around, along with trunks bearing stickers that charted journeys to and from India and Malaya and other outlying parts of the Empire.

I was greeted by the elderly receptionist, Enid, who was widely rumoured to be Rosa's daughter by Edward VII. I had been told this by mother who had also warned me on no account to make any reference to Evelyn Waugh's book, *Vile Bodies*, which was based on the hilarious sexual shenanigans at the Cavendish. It was banned and the mere mention of it would be enough to get you thrown out. As I checked in, Enid asked me if I was indeed Jack Salisbury's son, adding that if that were the case then Rosa herself would like to see me.

Rosa was then about ninety-three years old. I was shown into her private drawing room, where I was confronted by a lady still having the appearance of somebody from the Edwardian era. She was sitting bolt upright in a high-backed chair, enveloped in a huge blanket.

"This calls for wine," she announced, when I introduced myself. I had been told to expect this and that the wine was always champagne. If she liked you, the cost of the bottle would go on someone else's bill. If not, you would pay. It seemed that I passed muster because it was not included in my bill.

Years later, I related this story to a friend of my sister who had stayed there often. He nodded knowingly, adding that I probably hadn't realised that if she really, *really* liked you, she would supply a chorus girl too! Obviously, she must have only quite liked me.

During my stay I had lunch in the dining room and found myself reflecting that nothing much seemed to have changed there since the turn of the century – and that included the headwaiter. Towards the end of my meal, I noticed him counting out £5 notes from the cashbox and putting them into envelopes. It was a Friday, so I assumed he was making up the staff's weekly wages.

Then, suddenly, there appeared in the dining room an elderly red-faced gentleman, clad in an immaculate suit with a carnation in his buttonhole. Without a word, he picked his way rather unsteadily between the tables, walked up to where the headwaiter was counting out the money and reached past him to take a whole wad of notes out of the cashbox. Still without a word, he put the money in his jacket pocket, turned and weaved his way back through the tables, out of the dining room and out of the hotel. It had all been done quite openly and yet nobody seemed to have taken the slightest notice. People went on dining and waiters went about their business as if nothing untoward had happened. I seemed to be the only one who had noticed anything amiss.

When the headwaiter next passed my table I could contain myself no longer. "I hope you won't mind my mentioning it," I said, "but I could have sworn I just watched a gentleman come in and walk off with all the money out of your cash box. Or am I dreaming?"

The venerable figure of the headwaiter smiled down at me. "Oh, please don't worry about His Grace, Sir. He comes in every Friday for his weekend spending money and returns it all on Monday, plus an extra £5."

After I had been in Italy for about a year, the regiment was posted to Egypt, where Britain was embroiled in the problems associated with the emergence of the state of Israel. As we prepared to leave Italy, I was put in charge of the advance party responsible for assembling all the regiment's vehicles, including tanks, trucks and armoured personnel carriers, and getting them from Palmanova down to the docks in Venice to be loaded aboard the ship.

We were due to move out of the camp at 6.00am on the day of departure and by the previous evening I had completed all the arrangements and every vehicle was lined up, ready to go. The Colonel and the Adjutant, meanwhile, had all gone out to dinner, leaving me in charge as Orderly Officer. The Orderly Sergeant Major then approached me with a proposition. The Sergeants' Mess of an engineering regiment in the village were throwing a farewell party to which both he and I had been invited.

I had to reprimand the Sergeant Major, pointing out that, as he must have been perfectly well aware, neither of us, as Orderlies, must under any circumstances leave the camp. His response was to acknowledge that this was indeed true, whilst adding that it was a great pity that we wouldn't be able to go along as he had been reliably informed that the party was also going to be attended by a number of extremely beautiful and co-operative young Italian women. In the light of this most persuasive argument, I decided that we might be able to slip away for an hour – but no more than that.

We left at 7.00pm and on our return at 11.00pm I found myself confronted by an enraged Colonel and Adjutant. They had gone out to dinner secure in the knowledge that the Orderly Officer had everything in hand, fumed the Colonel. (I had, but not quite in the way he had envisaged!) He went on to explain through gritted teeth that at around 9.00pm, the General commanding the Army First Division had telephoned asking to speak to him. On being informed that he was out to dinner, the General then asked for the Adjutant, only to be told that, unfortunately, he, too, was out. The Orderly Officer? He could not be found. The Orderly Sergeant? Ditto.

When the Colonel returned from dinner to be given the message that the General had called, he duly rang back and had then been shocked to be subjected to a volley of verbals, suggesting, in no uncertain terms, that he seemed to have no control over his regiment. I now received an even worse dressing down. It ended with the Colonel saying that he had no doubt that I would make absolutely sure that nothing, but nothing, went wrong the next day and that the regiment would board the ship in an orderly and efficient manner.

I set off the next morning with egg all over my face, but quietly confident that I had done everything to ensure a model embarkation. I was still in a relaxed frame of mind when we arrived at the Venice docks to find the ship waiting to receive our vehicles and men, all of whom were present and correct. It was only when I was then asked for the boarding papers that I realised the one thing I had overlooked. No amount of pleading, bribery, anger or tears made any difference. No papers, no go.

I then had to drive all the way back to Palmanova, to report to the Colonel with the news that embarkation was delayed by a whole day, bracing myself for the monumental bollocking that ensued, along with the punishment of a depressingly large number of extra Orderly Officer duties – the equivalent, for a junior officer, of being confined to barracks. Armed with the necessary papers, I then drove back to Venice once again to supervise the embarkation under the contemptuous gaze of the men, most of whom were older and, I have to admit, probably a bit wiser than me.

I was still only nineteen at this stage and on a very steep learning curve in all sorts of ways. However, I was starting to grow up fast in the Army and the process was speeded up even further when the sophisticated off-duty pleasures of Venice and Trieste were replaced by something much earthier in Port Said, where the regiment was now based.

I was drinking with some fellow officers in the Port Said Officer's Club one evening when it was decided that we should go in search of some more exotic local nightlife. Leaving the Club, we hailed a gharry – a horse-drawn carriage – and simply told the driver to take us to a nightclub. Luckily, as it turned out, we shouted at our jeep driver to follow us.

The gharry then clip-clopped along, straight into the Arab Quarter. This was not a good idea. Post-war Port Said could be a very dangerous place if one strayed from the secure areas. The Arab Quarter was completely out of bounds. Stories of what happened to soldiers in there at night were frightening. Emboldened by our early evening drinks, however, we were in an adventurous mood as the gharry took us deeper and deeper into the foul-smelling labyrinth of back streets.

It eventually stopped outside a rather seedy-looking establishment, out of which appeared an enormous Arab woman with very large breasts that were threatening to spill out of a very low-cut gown. She beckoned us inside and I was first through the door, leaving my colleagues to pay off the gharry driver.

I found myself in a large bare room in which seven or eight large and rather unattractive Arab women were sitting. A flight of dimly lit stairs led up out of the room and tethered to the banister post was a donkey!

"You can have any of us," said one of the women.

"Thanks frightfully," I stammered, instantly getting cold feet as I appraised the situation. "But not tonight. I really must be off."

Absolutely no notice was taken of my polite refusal and, as I started to turn tail, I was grabbed by three of these appalling women and dragged upstairs, past the braying donkey. A door was thrown open and I was flung into bedroom, followed by a very fat woman, who locked the door behind her. She then hurled herself on the bed, pulled her dress over her head and bellowed: "OK! Ten bob."

In no mood to negotiate, I immediately offered her a £1 note to unlock the door.

On reaching the top of the stairs, I was confronted by the sight of my two brother officers being dragged upstairs by the other women, while the donkey, in a horrifying state of arousal, was braying with tremendous vigour. After a brief struggle, we all managed to fight our way out and jumped into the jeep beside our terrified driver. A very large brandy back at the Officers' Club helped to steady our nerves as we congratulated each other on our narrow escape from what we all agreed would probably have been a fate worse than death.

Meanwhile, my moral fortitude was also put to the test by my batman, a cockney named Mason. Choosing Mason was not popular with the other officers because up until then he had been designated Trooper I/C Officers' Ablutions. Friendly, cheerful and always optimistic, he made an ideal companion. And although disrespectful to virtually everyone else in authority, he was utterly loyal to me. On at least one occasion, he was a bit too assiduous in his efforts to look after me.

Shortly after the arrival in Port Said of our advance party, when we were living under canvas while we unloaded the transport that I had been detailed to bring over from Italy, he inquired what 'Sir' was intending to do that evening.

"Nothing much, I'm afraid, Mason," I told him. "I'm broke until next pay day."

He wandered off down the line of officers' tents, wearing a thoughtful frown on his face. When I returned to my tent that evening, I found to my surprise that my eveningwear had been neatly laid out, with the equivalent of £20 in local currency placed under my tunic.

I made no mention of this most welcome and unexpected windfall, but had the deepest suspicions about where it might have come from. A few days later, I managed to slip the same amount into Mason's kitbag in the hope that it would find its way back to wherever he had 'found' it. Mason, meanwhile, continued to be my batman, a perfect example of the sort of resourceful British serviceman who always succeeded in giving the impression of being unfazed by any crisis or danger.

I found this extremely comforting, especially as I seemed to be staggering from one crisis to the next. As if I hadn't had enough problems getting our tanks and other vehicles out of Italy, things got even worse when I found myself having to oversee their safe arrival and onward movement in Egypt.

While the rest of the regiment went to the barracks in Fyid, I remained in Port Said to supervise the unloading. My plan was to get the thirty tanks off first, my long-suffering Colonel having instructed me to make sure that they got priority.

Because the ship was not able to tie up right at the quayside, the unloading process involved winching the tanks down onto a fleet of lighters, which then ferried them ashore. At that point they had to be loaded onto railway transporters.

All was going well with the unloading onto the lighters until a fellow officer joined me at the ship's rail, from where I was directing operations, giving hand signals to the unsighted crane driver to indicate exactly when the tank was accurately positioned above the lighter and when to start and stop lowering. As I and the other officer became engrossed in our discussion about where we might dine that evening, I turned away from the rail while continuing to gesture to the crane driver to keep lowering. Unfortunately, with my attention distracted, I had failed to notice that the lighter had drifted out of position.

By the time I looked back, the tank was already disappearing beneath the surface of the water. The additional weight then snapped the chains and it sank to the bottom and was lost forever. And still the chapter of accidents was not complete.

Getting the tanks onto the railway trucks was no simple operation. The tank tracks actually overlapped the width of the flatbed trucks on either side, so it was necessary to stand in front and carefully direct each tank as it inched up the ramp and into position. To make things even more difficult, tanks do not have steering wheels, just joysticks on either side of the driver that effectively swivel it from left to right, so that there was very little margin for error.

With me standing there waving my arms and shouting "left hand down a bit" and "right hand down a bit", it took hours to load the twenty-nine tanks that had survived the transference from ship to shore, but we managed it in the end, a job well done. I was pretty pleased with myself and retreated to my office to ring the Colonel to tell him that his tanks would soon be on their way and would arrive the next day, somehow managing to gloss over the loss of the one that was on the seabed.

I had a very pleasant evening and slept well. The following afternoon a call came from the Colonel at headquarters and I answered brightly, in anticipation of a bit of praise for once. I will rephrase what he had to say, which was along the lines of: "Salisbury, you are a rather silly chap. My poor tanks have indeed arrived, but they cannot be taken off the train because you have put then on the wrong way round! So, with apologies for putting you to any inconvenience, I am sending them back to you so that you can try again. And by the way, I hope you will understand why I am giving you a further twenty Orderlies!"

From all of the foregoing, it will be obvious that I was perhaps not ideally suited to a military career. So when, in early 1948, the opportunity arose for me to leave with honour, I didn't hesitate. What happened was that after India was granted independence a lot of English officers in the Indian Army cavalry regiments had to be reassigned to English cavalry regiments. To make way for them, some of us were offered the choice of moving to another regiment or leaving altogether.

By then, I had already decided that I didn't like Army life enough to want to stay. Being an officer at that time was still a bit like being a member of a very exclusive club. You only mixed with people of your own class and kind, it was very stuffy and restrictive and there was a lot of snobbery, which I didn't like at all. So, I resigned my commission and set about finding something suitable in civvy street. Once again, grandpa Mitchelson came to the rescue.

# III

## DEB'S DELIGHT

As THE GRANDSON of the founder and former chairman, I didn't have too much difficulty fixing myself up with a job at Great Universal Stores. However, the family connection could not fast-track me to the higher echelons of the company and I started as a general trainee at £50-a-month, working in the linoleum department in the basement of the Mile End Road branch.

There were a couple of other employees in the department and our job was to hump the heavy rolls of lino around, unloading them from the trucks that brought them from the factory, putting them into store and then fetching them out, as required, for delivery to the customer. This, as you can imagine, was back-breaking work.

On my first day there, the other two very quickly sized me up. Both Cockneys, they had served as privates in the infantry during the war and, of course, my accent immediately marked me out as a toff from the officer classes.

Our opening conversation went something like this:

Private No 1: "Where'd you serve then, mate?"

Me: "Italy and Egypt."

Private No 2: "Yeah? What were you in, then?"

Me (hesitantly): "The cavalry, actually."

Private No 1: "An' what rank were you?

Me (even more hesitantly): "Me? Oh, Lieutenant."

I knew instantly that I was now in deep trouble. There was a long pause, during which the two men glanced at each other and exchanged knowing grins, before Private No 1 turned back to me and announced triumphantly: "Right, mate. You can pick up that roll of f****** lino behind you, stack it with that pile over there on the other side of the warehouse and then report back to us. And if you do it f****** right you can carry on doing the same f****** thing until the lunch break. OK?"

I doubt whether two ex-privates had ever had such a wonderful opportunity to wreak revenge for all the indignities suffered at the hands of officers during the war. However, once the novelty of being able to boss me about in a humiliating fashion had worn off, we actually became quite good mates and enjoyed the odd pint together after work.

Meanwhile, I didn't allow the lowliness of my position at work to cramp my social style. During my last few months in the Army in 1947 I had briefly experienced the very dubious pleasures of being a so-called Deb's Delight. For anyone not familiar with the formal workings of the pre-1960s social order, I should explain that this was the rather derogatory term used to describe those eligible young men from 'good' families who were approved as escorts to each year's crop of debutantes – well-bred young ladies who were 'coming out'.

Of course, 'coming out' did not then imply, as it probably would today, that the girls were revealing themselves as raging lesbians. Quite the opposite. It simply meant that at the age of seventeen or eighteen they were being formally launched into society, putting themselves in the shop window, as it were, in the hopes of attracting a suitably rich and well-connected husband. They would be presented at Court – and to the Cake at Queen Charlotte's Ball, which was hosted by Lady Howard de Walden. In between these two highlights there were numerous cocktail parties and dances as well as key sporting occasions such as Royal Ascot, Henley, Wimbledon, the Derby and the Eton v Harrow match at Lords. By the end of the 'season', many of the girls, often with the help of much scheming behind the scenes from socially ambitious mothers, would have succeeded in hooking a good catch.

It was as a result of my own mother's endeavours that I unfortunately found myself included in this dreadful charade as one of those on 'The List' of approved escorts and therefore in receipt of invitations to all the coming out parties. These were almost always mind-bogglingly and horrendously boring, especially the cocktail parties. Invariably held somewhere in Knightsbridge, they were attended by exactly the same people every time and always featured the same 'cocktail' – large jugs of pure orange juice with just the tiniest dash of gin added.

My friend Jan Barnes and I soon worked out a way of making these occasions a little more interesting. It was a simple three-point plan, the aim of which was: (1) to ingratiate ourselves with the hostess in the hope that she would report back favourably to our mothers and (2) to reverse the ratio of gin to orange in the drinks as a first step towards (3) encouraging a more positive response to our amorous advances from whichever of the female guests had taken our fancy.

The first stage was relatively easy. On being introduced to the hostess, who would invariably be holding one of the jugs of orange, you would say: "May I help you, Lady So-and-So?" before politely relieving her of the jug and proceeding to fill up a few glasses. Not only had you gained maximum Brownie points for politeness beyond the call of duty, but the jug was now firmly in your possession. This facilitated stages two and three. Surreptitiously taking flasks of gin from our pockets, we would slosh them into the jug before then homing in on the two most attractive, unattached girls in the room and plying them with the spiked orange. As the time to say our goodbyes and leave approached, we would then suggest moving on to an intimate dinner at one of our favourite restaurants, with the promise of dancing at a nightclub to follow.

Inevitably, it wasn't long before this ploy was rumbled. All it needed was for a couple of girls to report back to 'mummy', who complained to the hostess, who passed the complaint on to the List-Organiser-In-Chief, who then placed the letters USIT after my name – USIT standing for Unsafe In Taxis. At this point, the invitations ceased abruptly, for which I was extremely thankful, having already decided that this was not a social scene of which I really wanted to be part. It was time to move on.

With six friends, I had rented a house in Walton Street, just a few hundred yards from Harrods. The location was perfect. My only mistake was to be the one who actually signed the lease, thereby becoming responsible for any damages at the end of the tenure.

All but one of us were in our early twenties, the exception being Paddy Wells, a colourful Irish ex-fighter pilot who was about ten years our senior. Paddy had been wounded in the war and was in receipt of a disability pension that was conditional on him presenting himself every six months for a medical examination to confirm that he still qualified. This was always a very stressful time for Paddy since he was heavily dependent on the pension as the means to support his extremely active social life, which involved whisky, women and still more women.

To ensure that he was passed unfit on these occasions, he would take to the bottle the day before. In fact, he took to the bottle every day, but on the eve of the examination he would double his intake. It always worked. On presenting himself the following morning, his appearance alone would be enough to guarantee the continuation of the benefit payments.

My closest friends among the housemates were Jan Barnes and Roddy Wilson. We had been contemporaries at Eton and were also together in the Officer Cadet Training Unit. Roddy's father had fought with Glubb Pasha's legendary Arab Camel Legion in the Middle East and owned a dilapidated castle in Galloway. Roddy himself was a colourful, extrovert character who later became an inventor, travelling the world and getting involved in all sorts of interesting projects. In the Walton Street days he spent a lot of time experimenting with methods of growing mushrooms indoors. As this required soil, heat and damp conditions it is not hard to imagine the mess he created in every darkened space he could find.

Shortly after we had taken over the house, my sister, Jonet, who had just left school, asked if she could join us. A spirited girl, Jonet had had to be removed from several schools on account of her rebellious behaviour. This included climbing onto the roof at one genteel establishment and pelting the staff with apples from above. I thought it would be a great idea if she moved in with us, although it was highly unusual in those days for unmarried men and women to share accommodation. Even my mother, uninhibited as she was in many other respects, was against it, fearing that an attractive teenage girl could not possibly be safe living in a flat with a bunch of red-blooded young single males. It took a while to talk her round, but she did eventually agree.

As it happened, Jonet could not have been in safer hands. Not only was there an unspoken understanding among my friends that no one of them would ever dream of taking advantage of her; they also spontaneously formed a vigilant protective fence around her to fend off outsiders. Any new boyfriend who arrived to take her out would immediately be surrounded and subjected to an intense cross-examination about his intentions before being made very aware of the fact that if Jonet were to be upset or badly treated in any way, then he would have all of them to answer to. This prospect must have been just as frightening, if not more so, than anything that the sternest father could have threatened.

I have very fond recollections of the Walton Street period, despite the fact that we were permanently short of money. Things got so bad that at one point, during a particularly cold spell in the ferocious winter of 1952, we were reduced to chopping up the wooden steps leading down to the basement for use as firewood because we couldn't afford to buy coal. Our lack of funds was not because we didn't have jobs or allowances. We simply spent every penny we had on parties and nightclubs.

Post-war London may have been rather drab in some respects, but there was still plenty of fun for those who could afford it – and even for some, like us, who very often could not. We regularly had to resort to some quite imaginative ploys to raise the necessary cash. In my own and Jonet's case, this usually involved milking the Trust Fund that grandpa had set up on our behalf. The terms of the Trust dictated that we couldn't start to receive an annual income from it until we were twenty-one. However, the Trustees were empowered to authorise certain necessary expenditure relating to things like clothing and medical expenses. To take full advantage if this loop-hole, one first had to convince the Trust, in the form of a Welsh solicitor called Mr Pratt, of the validity of one's claim. Mr Pratt was a very serious man, with no sense of humour and a deep suspicion of almost anything I was associated with. In other words, he did exactly the job my grandfather would have wanted.

One scheme that worked very well, but which could only be used sparingly, involved making a visit to my tailor, Huntsman in Savile Row, where I would purchase, say, three raincoats and two umbrellas, with the bill going direct to the Trust. I would then sell the surplus items to my friends at a handsome discount for cash.

Jonet then won my undying admiration by managing to pull off an even more audacious scam. In a moment of dire need, she concocted a story about a dreadful accident that she had suffered while walking down the King's Road, in Chelsea. This supposedly involved tripping over a kerb, falling flat on her face and knocking out all her front teeth. Extensive and very expensive dentistry was urgently required to repair the damage, she pleaded tearfully over the phone to Mr Pratt, her mouth stuffed full of marbles to add dramatic effect.

One way and another, all of us somehow regularly managed to scrape together enough money to keep up appearances as gay young blades about town. The fashionable nightclubs that we frequented at the time included the Milroy, where Paul Adams and Edmundo Ros were the resident bandleaders, the Orchid Room and the Jacaranda. The latter opened, very conveniently, just around the corner from the Walton Street house only three months after we moved in, with Prince Philip as the first member and me as the fourth! The smart places to eat were the Berkeley Grill, Quaglinos and the Bagatelle. And we spent far too much time in favourite pubs such as The Star Tavern in Belgrave Mews, the Antelope and the Duke of Wellington in Eaton Terrace and the Hereford Arms, just off Gloucester Road.

The Hereford Arms was especially popular since the landlord, Bill Bell-Syre, was a jovial, extrovert and extremely generous character, always very understanding about cashing cheques that he knew would bounce if he presented them before the end of the month! He also had the capacity to make serious inroads into the pub's supply of gin all by himself. This had the rather unusual effect of causing his conversation to lapse intermittently and without any warning into slurred gibberish. His regulars were so used to this that whoever chanced to be standing nearest to him at the time would lean over, tap him on the shoulder and shout: "Oi, Bill, you've gone again!" Whereupon he would immediately strike himself extremely hard across the face and go back to talking perfectly lucidly, as if nothing had happened.

At one point, Bill installed a pinball machine in the bar. I was idly playing it one evening when a man sauntered across and started watching. After a while I became aware that he was standing a mite too close to my left hand and was brushing against it as I thumped the button on the machine.

At that moment, Bill's voice called out from behind the bar. "Tony, go to the heads!" I hadn't the slightest idea what he meant and assumed he was probably having one of his turns. "Go to the heads, Tony," he repeated. I ignored him, but stopped playing the machine because the man beside me was now pressing himself against me in a manner that clearly suggested he was up to no good.

I retreated to the bar, at which point Bill came up and muttered: "Will you go to the heads, for Christ's sake!"

"I haven't a clue what you're talking about, Bill," I replied innocently.

"It means go to the lavatory, you idiot," he hissed, with mounting exasperation. Being an Army man, I had no idea that 'the heads' was a naval term for the loo.

"Why the hell should I?" I persisted, still puzzled. "I don't need a pee at the moment."

"Look," whispered Bill. "That bloke who's been standing next to you comes in here every year during the motor show. I know exactly what he's up to and I intend to catch him at it."

My jaw dropped and I looked at him in horror. "Are you telling me, Bill, that you want to set me up and allow me to be accosted in the lavatory by some chap who might come from Birmingham, for all I know!" I stuttered.

He gave me a hurt look. "Well, I wouldn't have allowed it to go too far before I broke it up," he said in a tone that suggested he felt I was letting the side down.

The landlord of The Star Tavern, Paddy Kennedy, was very different to Bill, revelling in his reputation as the rudest publican in London. The pub itself was also fairly notorious. This was largely because of the upstairs saloon bar, which, although open to all, had the slightly threatening atmosphere of a rather seedy but exclusive club, the clientele consisting mainly of film starlets, minor celebrities, well-known gangsters and other assorted dodgy characters. As a result, the goings-on there frequently attracted the attention of the national Press, particularly the gossip column of the *Daily Express*.

Members of the smart young social set were drawn to the place by its louche reputation. Debs loved being taken there for the excitement, and for the chance of overhearing the sort of language that they only normally encountered out on the hunting field! The only other reason for putting up with Paddy Kennedy's unpleasantness, not to mention the large Alsatian dog that he kept behind the bar, was that official opening hours varied from one local district to the next in those days and closing time at The Star was half-an-hour later than at The Antelope and the Duke of Wellington.

After an evening at the cinema, a friend and I emerged at 10.15pm in dire need of a drink and made a bee-line for The Star, which closed at 11.00pm rather than 10.30pm. We arrived in good time and ordered two pints, only to be refused by Curly, the downstairs barman, who informed us that he had just been ordered not to serve any more drinks and to clear everyone out. It seemed that Paddy had decided he was fed up with people only coming in from other pubs at 10.30pm so that they could enjoy an extra half-an-hour's drinking.

For some reason, I was absolutely incensed about this. I have always been the most mild-mannered of men, hating rows of any kind. But on this occasion I decided to make a stand, especially surprising given that I hadn't had a drink all night.

"Ridiculous," I exploded, adding rather pompously: "I'm going to phone the police right away to complain."

The public phone was at the top of the stairs, just outside the door leading to the select bar. Curly must have sent word up to Paddy on the intercom to let him know what was going on because just as I picked up the receiver the door to the bar opened and out came a very large, well-built and extremely tough-looking middle-aged man who proceeded to ask me, with an air of quiet menace, what I thought I was doing.

I had no idea at this stage that this gentleman was none other than Eddie Chapman, a well-known villain who had served several long prison sentences for safe-breaking and various other misdemeanours. He had been recruited as a spy during the war and went over to Germany where he posed as a double agent, whereas in fact he was a triple agent for Britain. Had I known all this, then my answer to his inquiry about what I was doing would have been something along the lines of "not a lot", followed by a hasty retreat. Instead of which I said defiantly: "I'm calling the police to complain about Paddy."

"I don't think so, mate," he murmured and knocked me down the stairs.

Up until that moment, I had never been hit quite like that and, apart from the pain, the shock was considerable. I ended up at the bottom of the stairs, slightly dazed, while a deafening silence settled over the ground floor bar as eighty or so interested onlookers waited with bated breath to see what would happen next.

Without really thinking, I automatically allowed the old public school code of honour to take over; stand up for yourself, don't lose face and, above all, be brave. I slowly hauled myself up the stairs again. On reaching the top and being confronted with my assailant, I looked him straight in the eye and said, in my best Old Etonian voice: "I wouldn't do that again, if I were you."

Seconds later, I once again picked myself up from the floor at the bottom of the stairs. I dusted myself down and, with the bar still in complete silence, I walked unsteadily, but with my head held high, out of The Star Tavern and into the night.

The Star wasn't the only place where I found myself out of my depth. At the other end of the social scale, at the Jacaranda, I became deeply smitten by the beautiful top fashion model who was the co-owner of the club. I eventually plucked up the courage to ask her out to dinner and, much to my surprise, she accepted.

On the appointed evening, I donned my dinner jacket, as one did in those days, bought some flowers and went to pick her up at her flat. This was located in a very smart block somewhere in Knightsbridge. As I stood waiting for the lift, another chap arrived, also in a dinner jacket and also with a bouquet of flowers. We nodded at each other and, when the lift arrived, both got in together. I pressed the button for the third floor, he watched me and did nothing. We both got out. Her flat was down the corridor to the right, so I stepped that way and stood at the door. So did he. At this point I couldn't help noticing that he was exceptionally well attired, a bit older than me and extremely confident in his manner, with flowers that definitely put mine in the weed class. Without a word, I presented him with my pathetic bunch of wilting blooms and left.

I suffered an even more embarrassing reverse when I set my sights on a stunning girl whom I met at a cocktail party. Although she was somewhat intense about the Arts, her beauty and figure inspired me with the confidence to believe that I would be able to busk it, even if the conversation moved slightly out of my intellectual reach.

It appeared that she was besotted with Myra Hess, who, I soon discovered, was to appear the following week at the Royal Albert Hall. Since Miss Hess was neither a well-known cricketer nor an entertainer in the popular style of Bing Crosby, I knew nothing about her. I certainly had no idea that she was arguably the most famous classical pianist in the world at the time. This, however, did not deter me from booking a box at the Albert Hall and then nonchalantly inviting the object of my affections to join me for the concert.

She was over the moon and I set about making my plans for the evening – champagne in the box, an orchid, an intimate table in a quiet corner of my favourite restaurant and then a nightclub. At the same time, I spent at least two days frantically trying to borrow enough money to finance this grand seduction!

The evening came. I collected her. She looked even more ravishing than ever. We arrived at the Albert Hall. We were escorted to our box. The champagne was opened. The curtain was about to go up.

As the lights went down I turned to the radiant beauty I was trying so hard to impress and asked brightly: "So, what do you think she's going to be singing tonight, then?"

I can remember only one other occasion from this period of my life when I felt more of a fool. The story starts, as so often at that time, at a cocktail party. I found myself chatting to a couple of blokes about the Oxford and Cambridge boat race, which was still one of the biggest events in the British sporting calendar in those days. I was holding forth on the prospects of the respective crews and must have sounded fairly convincing because one of these chaps then asked whether I rowed myself.

Emboldened by several stiff gin-and-tonics and getting quite carried away with myself by this point, my response, despite the fact that I had never picked up an oar in anger, was an incredulous: "Yes, of course. I've rowed all my life, for God's sake!"

The two men glanced at each other and one asked rather tentatively: "Then I suppose you are already involved with a club in the Head of the River Race?"

I hadn't a clue what they were talking about, but realised that I had already passed the point of no return. "As a matter of fact, no," I replied, as nonchalantly as possible. "I haven't actually got around to joining a club yet."

"Ah! Well in that case I wonder whether you might consider being part of our eight? We're not awfully good – in fact, we're on the lowest rung of the ladder at the Leander Rowing Club. But it's just a bit of fun really, nothing too serious. So, how about it?

"Delighted," I heard myself saying.

"We'll be contacting you very shortly," I was told.

I thought no more about it. A few weeks later they rang me to say how pleased they were that I had indicated my willingness to be part of their crew and that they could now confirm my selection. I was told to present myself at the Putney Boat House at 10.30am on the morning of the race.

It was only now that I began to have vague misgivings about what I had got myself into. After all, the event, featuring crews from all over the country, was taking place on the morning of the Boat Race itself, and over the same Mortlake to Putney course. But, amazingly, I still thought I might be able to busk my way out of trouble.

Apart from the fact that I had never rowed in my life, except as a child on the Serpentine, I didn't even have any proper kit. As soon as I arrived at the boathouse wearing my cricket flannels, sweater and plimsolls the true enormity of the situation began to dawn on me. And yet still I tried to bluff it out.

The place was teeming with the fittest looking men I had even seen. I eventually located my crew, who were limbering up with frightening enthusiasm while making remarks like: "Gosh, I won't half be glad to be out of training for a while after this." I let the cigarette slip unnoticed from my hand and stepped on it.

There was then a move to the boathouse to collect our craft. There were dozens of the things racked above our heads. The whole place was a hive of frantic activity as the various eights collected their respective boats. We lined up under ours, with me just tagging along, watching what everybody else was doing and trying to follow suit. A voice cried 'Up!' at which point seven pairs of hands shot under the boat, followed, a fraction of a second later, by mine.

We lifted the thing off its rack and marched it down to the jetty. Another 'Up!' and it was deftly turned over and placed in the water.

"Are you happy at No 3, Tony?" inquired the Cox. As it happened, I always batted at No 3 when playing cricket, so that seemed rather appropriate. I mumbled my agreement, not knowing which end of the blasted thing to count from. I just waited until everyone else was in position and then climbed into the vacant space. Before doing so, I noticed that all the others had taken off their shoes, which seemed rather strange. Once again, however, I simply followed suit.

I found myself sitting on a very unstable, slithery seat with what looked like a pair of clogs for my feet.

"I presume you're alright with a sliding seat?" inquired a voice as I slid back and sideways.

"No problem", I retorted nervously as I tried to manoeuvre the heavy and extremely unwieldy oar into position in the rowlock.

Everyone else was quietly settled as the other boats went off to row the four-and-half-miles down to the start line at Mortlake. Shouts of command, quite incomprehensible to me, were coming from the various Coxes to their crews. Everything seemed in good order. Then the time came for us to get going.

I thought I heard the Cox say: "Push off." So, I jabbed my oar into the jetty to do exactly that.

"Don't do that, No 3," he shouted. "We don't want to upset the boat."

We sat there, sort of drifting, and then the Cox suddenly shouted: "READY!" Everyone gripped their oar and leaned forward. I tried to do the same, but my seat slid out of control, my feet slipped out of the clogs, and I found myself falling backwards rather than leaning forwards.

"Please pull yourself together, No 3 – I'm about to get testy!"

growled the Cox, who, up until that moment, had seemed quite a pleasant chap.

He tried again: "READY!" This time we all tensed as one. "ROW!" he bellowed. The blade of my oar bit deep into the water while the handle thundered back, striking me in the solar plexus. And, again, my feet became un-clogged.

"For Christ's sake, No 3, do you realise that all the other boats are halfway to Mortlake and we will now have to race to get to the start in time for the race itself! Now, are you ready?"

I nodded weakly – and immediately caught another crab. "Have you never rowed a boat before?" queried the Cox in what I thought was an unreasonably sarcastic voice.

"Well, no actually. Very sorry and all that."

"Dear God," groaned the Cox, his head in his hands. I thought he might be crying.

At that moment, and I swear this is true, another member of the crew suddenly hailed a cyclist on the towpath. "Is that you, Freddie?"

"It is indeed," yelled back the cyclist.

"Well, can you do us a very, very big favour?"

"If I can. Sure."

"Great! Well, could you get off your bike, swim out here and change places with the **** at No 3?"

"OK," agreed Freddie, abandoning his cycle, taking off his shoes and sweater and then half-wading, half-swimming out to the boat.

Not a word was spoken as I climbed out and went back the way he had come. Not daring to take his bike, I squelched back to the main road, where it took me an hour to find a taxi driver prepared to allow my bedraggled figure into his cab and to deliver me to the Hereford Arms. There, I borrowed enough money to pay him off and drink myself into oblivion. I never heard another thing from the two chaps who had recruited me, but, all these years later, I still have nightmares about the shame of it all.

Apart from that incident and those few minor setbacks on the romantic front, I was having a ball. At Walton Street there was never a dull moment. I had got to know some of the musicians in the resident six-piece band at the Jacaranda and one Saturday evening I invited them to come over to the house after they had finished at the club to join us at a bottle party we were holding. One thing led to another and after being plied with liquor they ended up jamming together until the early hours of the morning, while the rest of us danced to the music. This was such a success all round that it became a regular Saturday night event from midnight to about 3.00am, the band happy to play for nothing except free drinks.

On these occasions we always tried to keep the number of guests down to about thirty, but as word got around we began to get quite a few gatecrashers. There was one night when I had to bar a very drunken friend, who immediately went off to Piccadilly in high dudgeon, picked up the most horrible, aged prostitute he could find and returned to the house. Luckily, it was I, once again, who happened to answer the doorbell. Hoping to avoid a scene, I welcomed them both and then quickly ushered her upstairs, telling her to take off her coat and wait while I found her a drink. I then rushed down, grabbed an empty Gordon's gin bottle and filled it with water before taking it up to her with the suggestion that she might like to get stuck into it while her friend got himself sorted out downstairs.

Moments later, there was an explosion of cursing and swearing from inside the room, followed by the lady's appearance in the doorway, clutching the bottle and launching into a stream of abuse, the general gist of which was something along the lines of: "With respect, sir, I would prefer not to waste any more of my valuable time in an establishment that provides its guests with cheap, watered-down alcohol."

She then stormed out, just as I had anticipated she would. No-one else was aware of the incident and my friend was so drunk that he fell asleep almost immediately and woke up on the sofa the next morning with a serious headache but no recollection of what had happened the night before.

Life continued in this pleasantly aimless and rather dissolute way for the next four or five years, my fairly meagre wages now supplemented by my income from the Trust. In addition to my busy weekday social activities in the West End, I was now spending every summer weekend in the country in East Sussex, having picked up the threads of my school cricketing career to become a regular and enthusiastic member of the historic Rottingdean village team.

I was then rather unexpectedly shaken out of this comfortable routine by the news that GUS wanted to transfer me to Manchester. I reacted with undisguised horror. As far as I was concerned, this was the British equivalent of being banished to the salt mines of Siberia. Never mind North of Watford – I wasn't sure if civilisation extended much beyond Swiss Cottage! Lord's cricket ground was about as far as I ventured had in that direction. Rather than submit to such a drastic relocation, I decided to resign and seek alternative employment.

This, as it turned out, marked the beginning of the end of my salad days. I was about to come down to earth with a bang.

# IV

## DOWN – AND OUT – IN THE ROCKIES

O N LEAVING Great Universal Stores in 1952, I applied to join the Rank Organisation. I was taken on as a trainee cinema manager and sent off to the Astoria in Streatham. In those days, cinema managers and their deputies wore dinner jackets in the evenings. As it turned out, the dress code was just about the only way in which I had any sort of affinity with the job. What I hadn't appreciated until it was too late was that it required one to be on duty not only every evening, but also at weekends, over Bank Holidays and even at Christmas, thereby putting paid to just about all my social and cricketing activities. Apart from that, it was not a particularly pleasant place to work even at the best of times.

Saturday mornings, when hordes of dreadful, screaming children descended on the cinema, were especially horrific. The little blighters would be everywhere, causing havoc – in the foyer, in the lavatories, climbing over the seats and trying to get on stage. Any attempt to restore some sort of order was fatal, only making matters worse. Even when they had sort of settled down and had ceased cat-calling and pelting the manager, who was simply trying to tell them what they were about to see, the noise never abated. The usual cowboy flicks might as well have been silent movies for all that you could hear of the soundtrack.

I was just thankful that I did not have to get involved in the clearing up afterwards. The removal of chewing gum from every available surface in the auditorium was a particularly unpleasant and almost impossible task that was never carried out very effectively, with the result that later audiences inevitably ended up with the disgusting stuff sticking like glue to their clothes and their shoes.

Despite all this, the kids' matinee was regarded by the management as an essential part of the weekly programme. The kids loved it, the parents were thrilled to have the children off their hands for a couple of hours and the public relations value to the cinema chain was considerable.

The older youngsters were even worse. This was the height of the Teddy Boy era and although they are looked back on as an amusing part of the social change at the time, with their almost comically theatrical garb of drape jackets, tight trousers, crepe-soled shoes and bootlace ties, quite a large proportion of them were dangerous thugs who carried cut-throat razors and flick knives as the weapons of choice. I certainly felt less than totally comfortable going home on a bus at 11.30pm each night in a dinner jacket.

Fred Archer, the cinema manager, had previously run the Odeon in Leicester Square and was therefore very experienced. When the Teds started slashing the seats, insulting the usherettes and frightening the more respectable customers, he decided to take action. One Sunday he called me into his office and announced: "Right. As from tonight we are banning all Teddy Boys."

By the time we were ready to open the doors, there was a queue stretching right around the building, consisting mostly of Teds in full regalia. I started to back away. "Where do you think you're going," demanded Fred.

"I thought I might take refuge in the toilets for a few hours," I replied.

"You get back here," ordered Fred. "There's nothing to worry about. Watch me. I know how to handle this. For a start, we are going to open just a single door, so that they can only get in one by one."

I went out and stood very much behind him. He opened the door and each time a Teddy Boy tried to enter he said in a very commanding voice: "Sorry, mate. You lot are all banned until you learn to behave yourselves."

To my amazement they all meekly complied, shrugging their padded shoulders and ambling off without a hint of trouble.

After a few minutes, Fred said: "OK, that's it. I'm going for a cup of tea. You take over."

I blanched and started moving away again. "Come on, now," said Fred. "Just do exactly as I did and you'll be fine."

Trying hard to remember my Army training, I stood alone at the door as the queue shuffled forward and immediately experienced a sinking feeling as the next Teddy Boy in line approached. He was at least six-foot-six tall, with bushy eyebrows, a curled lip and shoulders about a yard wide. Drawing myself to attention, I said in my best public school voice: "I'm terribly sorry, old chap, but I'm afraid we are unable to let you in tonight. I do hope you understand."

There was a long silence as the giant Ted considered this while, behind him, the rest of the queue looked on expectantly. I braced myself for what I thought was an almost inevitable assault. I couldn't help noticing what looked suspiciously like the handle of a cut-throat razor protruding from the breast pocket of his jacket. Suddenly, his right hand moved upwards. It all seemed to happen in slow motion. However, instead of going for the razor, the hand reached into his inner pocket and came out clutching a handkerchief. He blew his nose.

"OK, Guv. If you say so," he muttered, shrugging his immense shoulders and slouching away.

I tried not to let my relief show and handled the rest of the queue with renewed confidence.

Despite gradually getting to grips with the demands of the job, I soon realised that cinema management was not for me, especially as my social life was becoming virtually non-existent as a result of the hours I had to keep. So I resigned − and went off to explore Canada.

That may seem a rather extreme reaction − and, of course, there was actually more to it than mere disillusionment with my career prospects in this country. I thought the time was right to see a bit more of the world.

I had no particular reason for choosing Canada, apart from a vague idea that I might still be able to get the odd game of cricket, having heard that there were quite a few ex-pat teams operating out there. I had no fixed plan of action and no job to go to. I didn't even know anybody out there. I simply booked a berth on the ship from Southampton and hoped that something would turn up once I got there.

I arrived first in Montreal and then took a train all the way across the country to Vancouver. That part of the journey was an experience in itself. For several days I found myself in a compartment with a selection of DPs (Displaced Persons) from all over Europe. They had primus stoves, accordions and guitars and were thoroughly enjoying themselves on what was, for all of us in our different ways, I guess, a big adventure. Once I got used to what seemed like the distinct possibility of being burned alive in a railway carriage as a result of an exploding primus stove, I found it all enormously exhilarating, even though the language barrier was a big drawback.

On arrival in Vancouver I had just $50, which went on two weeks' advance rent for a small bedsit in a poorish district. This was March, it was still snowing heavily and the temperature was positively Arctic. Urgently in need of employment of some kind if I was not to end up on the streets, I presented myself at the Labour Exchange the very next day. There, I joined a long queue of DPs. After about an hour I got to the head of the queue and was asked what I was looking for in the way of a job.

"Anything you've got going," I replied. "I'm pretty desperate."

"I don't think we've got anything that would suit you," said the official, eyeing me dubiously and clearly recognising my public school accent.

"I'm really not fussy," I insisted.

"Well, they need people to lay drains for a storm sewer just outside the city," he said, adding rather ominously: "It pays $3-an-hour, but I don't think you'll last long so I'll keep an eye out for something a bit more suitable."

"Thanks a lot. When do I start?" I asked enthusiastically.

"You will be picked up on the corner of Marks Street at 6.30am," I was told. "And, by the way, how much money have you got?"

"About $12," I replied.

To my astonishment, he said immediately: "That's not enough. Here's $50 to tide you over. Pay me back whenever you can." It was an incredible act of kindness, generosity and trust, the like of which I can't recall ever having experienced at any other time, before or since.

Meanwhile, I still had another small problem. When I left England, the one thing I had not envisaged was that I would be laying sewer drains for a living and I had certainly not had the foresight to visit my tailor in Savile Row with a request to kit me out for such activity! All I had that was remotely practical were my cricket flannels, boots and sweater.

I therefore cut a somewhat incongruous figure as I waited on the street corner for the truck to pick me up. There were about fifteen of us altogether, a mixture of Germans, Poles, Hungarians and other refugees from all over Europe. The truck was open-backed and the temperature was about ten degrees below zero.

By the time we reached the site, a desolate location about ten miles outside Vancouver, I felt as if I was already suffering from advanced hypothermia. And the scene that now confronted me did not help to raise my spirits one little bit. I found myself staring into a large, deep and seemingly endless trench, at the bottom of which enormous drainpipes were in the process of being laid.

The foreman called us all together and told us that our job would be to clear out the slushy, frozen water that had gathered in the trench so that the next lot of pipes could go in. Then, looking me up and down with a rather quizzical expression on his face − as well he might, given what I was wearing − he drawled: "Are you English?"

I told him that, yes, actually I was. "Well, get your ass down that hole, grab a spade and start digging," he ordered.

There was a ladder that all the others were using to climb down into the trench. It seemed pretty obvious that the foreman had already got me down in his own mind as a delicate flower who would not be up to doing the work required so, hoping to prove him wrong, I ignored the ladder and jumped down into the trench.

It took four people to pull me out. I had landed in a spot where the heavy, slushy, icy mud was about four feet deep and I sank up to my thighs. It was not a happy start.

I found a spade and started digging. After what seemed like about two hours, but was probably more like fifteen minutes, the foreman reappeared above me and shouted: "Hey, Limey – I need you to crawl up that drainpipe and clear all the rubbish out that has collected there."

I crawled into this bloody great pipe in my sodden, muddy cricket gear and having got about five or six yards into it, with icy water pouring down my shirt and lumps of freezing slush sticking all over me, I began to get cramp in both legs. I had never felt quite so miserable in my entire life and became convinced that this was going to be the end of me, fearing that I was about to be cut off in my prime in the most inglorious circumstances.

All I could think of was my mother, who was the most terrible snob, having to tell all her posh friends: "I'm afraid Anthony died in a drain in Canada."

In fact, I somehow survived this ordeal for another ten days before I went back to the friendly official at the Labour Exchange and admitted defeat. He was most sympathetic and said that, as it happened, something had come up that he felt would be much more suitable. He then sent me off for an interview with a company that sold magazine subscriptions door-to-door. Their main titles were *Colliers*, *The Red Book* and *Good Housekeeping*.

At the interview, the Sales Manager explained that he had a team of six people working for him – five of whom, it later turned out, had prison records. The company paid neither a salary nor even commission. The way their system worked was that if you were successful in getting a housewife to take out a year's subscription, you had to get your commission from her in the form of so-called 'front money'. This supposedly guaranteed that she would then get the magazines at a heavily discounted price. In fact, she ended up paying more than they cost on the bookstalls.

We were carefully trained to use a formal sales technique. You were sent out to cover a certain area, armed with samples of each of the three magazines. You would knock on the door and, when it was opened, hold out the samples and say: "Good morning, madam – you haven't been receiving your share of these samples." When she stretched out her hand to take the samples, you were then supposed to hold on to them firmly while you went into your spiel.

On my first morning in the job I set off without much enthusiasm and after walking miles to reach my designated 'patch', went up to the door of the first house and rang the bell. After a short interval it was answered by a woman who took one look at me and, before I even had time to open my mouth, said: "Nothing today, thank you" and went to close the door.

"But I say, Madam," I piped up hurriedly, proffering my samples. "You haven't been receiving your share of these samples."

"Oh, thanks very much," she said, snatching them out of my hand and then slamming the door in my face.

With nothing left to sell, I had to trudge about five miles back to base to collect more samples. I got a bollocking from the sales manager and then had to flog all the way out again. I decided I had been happier down the sewer.

The set spiel I had been taught simply wasn't working and I couldn't even get a sniff of a sale. What's more, the rudeness of people was extremely upsetting at times. There was so much door-to-door selling in Canada that people there were hardened to it.

After a very short time, I developed my own sales pitch, which at least achieved a bit more than the official company line. For instance, having realised that a high proportion of residents were immigrants from UK, I would announce as soon the door was opened: "Good morning, Madam, I'm just over from England." Many of these women were longing to talk to someone fresh from the old country and I was invariably invited in for a cup of tea. And even if I didn't make a sale, it was just nice to sit down and relax for a few minutes.

My other approach was much more pathetic, but very successful on at least two occasions. It went like this: Rude, unpleasant woman snaps: "Not today, thank you" and slams the door. I then proceed to scream: "Oh, my God! My thumb, my thumb," making as if it has got caught in the door and I am in agony. The door opens again. "Oh, you poor boy! I'm so sorry. Do come in and I'll bathe it for you."

This would give me the perfect opportunity to go into a long sob story about how I had just arrived from England, all alone and with no money and how, if I didn't make a sale, I would be out on the streets. As I say, it worked well on a couple of occasions.

However, after a few generally unproductive and totally soul-destroying weeks, I finally gave it up as another bad job and decided to move on, this time to Calgary, a thousand miles away. I managed to hitch a lift from Vancouver with a young man whom I knew only slightly and that turned out to be yet another – almost terminal – mistake. Our route across the Rocky Mountains, via Kicking Horse Pass, took us through some of the most spectacular scenery I have ever seen. The problem was that my chauffeur sprouted horns as soon as he got behind the wheel of his Cadillac and drove like a complete maniac. I was petrified all the way up to Banff, where, as he had been threatening to do from the moment we set off, he lost control, careered off the road at speed and turned the car over in the most terrifying fashion.

I was extremely fortunate to crawl out of the wreckage without a scratch, but he was not so lucky, losing an eye in the accident. While he was carted off to hospital, I then managed to cadge another lift for the last hundred miles or so to Calgary.

In 1954, Calgary was something of a boomtown, growing incredibly fast as the business and administrative centre for the Canadian oil industry, with the oil wells themselves based mostly around Edmonton, four hundred miles away.

Having found myself some cheap lodgings, I set out the next day to find employment.

It was now that I got my first taste of Canadian cricket. I was pleasantly surprised to find that there were no less than seven very active clubs in Calgary and I wasted no time in joining one of them. My team were a real mixed bunch that included a Japanese wicket keeper, whose blood-curdling shouts of 'Howzat!' for catches and stumpings were extremely unnerving for one and all, being delivered in very shrill, high-pitched scream that was more like a war cry than an appeal.

However, the grounds were very attractive, the pitches excellent and the general standard of play much higher than I had expected. I managed to acquit myself fairly well and after only a month I was selected to represent the Province of Alberta against the Province of British Columbia in a match at Edmonton.

This was considered a very important fixture, as there was a long history of fierce rivalry between Alberta and British Columbia. It was, I suppose, the Canadian equivalent of a Roses match between Yorkshire and Lancashire.

Our team was made up of five Englishmen, four Canadians, two Americans and the Japanese wicket keeper. Our skipper, one of the Canadians, was very serious, very keen and – God help us! – a teetotaller. The English contingent, in particular, were horrified to discover, when we arrived in Edmonton, that he had booked us into a Temperance hotel.

This called for immediate action. We decided that two of us would slip out of the hotel, visit a liquor store and smuggle back essential supplies of brandy, scotch, gin and beer. This mission was achieved successfully and the contraband was hidden in one of our rooms while we went downstairs for a team dinner washed down with lemonade and mineral water. As if that were not enough of an ordeal, we then had to sit through an embarrassing team talk from our captain, during which he did his best to impress upon us that the honour of Alberta was at stake.

The 'Limeys' couldn't wait to escape to the 'drinks room' for some serious liquid refreshment. To add to the party atmosphere, one of our number had somehow arranged for three nurses from the local hospital to join us – though how he managed to smuggle them past reception remains a mystery.

At about three o'clock in the morning, the three who had managed to pair off with the nurses sneaked off to their respective rooms, leaving myself and the other remaining Brit to polish off what was left of the booze. In the end, I had about two hours sleep before coming down to breakfast in less than brilliant form.

"You look dreadful," said the captain, eyeing me suspiciously. "You haven't by any chance been drinking, have you?"

"Drinking?" I replied. "Never stopped since nine o'clock last night. Wonderful evening. Woke up in the shower half-an-hour ago."

"You do realise, don't you, that you will be representing the Province of Alberta in three hours time?" he growled, in a dangerously low voice.

He went on: "You are the main batsman, going in at No 3, and a lot is resting on your shoulders. If things go wrong, it will probably be due to your condition."

There was no support forthcoming from my new-found English mates, who were all looking down sheepishly at their fried eggs. I tried to draw myself up to a fully upright position, which proved almost impossible thanks to the hammers beating inside my skull.

"Now look here, skip," I bleated. "You don't know me. I am always at my best with a hangover. It helps to steady the nerves and encourages you to keep your head down. So, have no fear. All will be well."

"F****** right, it will!" he bellowed, his tone of voice changing alarmingly. "This ****** match is too ****** important for a ****** Limey to **** it up." For a Temperance man with high religious beliefs, he seemed unduly agitated.

We arrived at the ground, which was very imposing and ringed by an unexpectedly large number of spectators. We fielded first and were left to get a reasonable target of 265 to win. Unfortunately, we then lost a wicket in the first over, which meant that I was in a little earlier than I had hoped. As I picked up my bat and prepared to walk out to the wicket, the captain came up and it was quite obvious that he couldn't make up his mind whether to threaten all sorts of retribution if I failed or try to fill me with quiet, confident encouragement. Before he had time to make up his mind, I was on my way.

There are some occasions when you go in to bat with a feeling of absolute certainty that this is going to be your day. This was just such an occasion. I took guard, looked around the field and settled into my stance, ready to receive the first ball.

It was an absolute gift, gentle medium pace, on a length and dead straight – just the kind of thing you want to get you off the mark. I played forward confidently ... and missed. Behind me there was that awful dry rattle and my middle stump toppled over. As the opposition celebrated, I could sense the silence from the pavilion. I could also imagine the profanities that would be issuing from the captain's mouth once he had recovered from the initial shock. For the only time in my entire cricketing career I decided not to walk straight back to the pavilion as the umpire raised his finger. Instead, I walked off the pitch in the opposite direction and cowered behind a tree.

When I did eventually dare to show my face the captain couldn't

*"Tall, slim ... and very imposing"* – *my mother,*
(ABOVE) *relaxing by the swimming pool; with my*
*grandparents, Sir Archie and Lady Mitchelson*
(RIGHT), *and* (BELOW) *with her second husband, my*
*stepfather Alex Barclay, in Cannes in 1934.*

TOP: *A visit to the pyramids. My mother is on the camel and I'm in the trap with a hanky on my head. Next to me is nanny Bubba while Jonet is in the arms of a servant.*

*My mother's family home in Sussex* (ABOVE) *and* (RIGHT) *Alex Barclay, a leading international polo player, receiving the Wimbledon Cup from the Duchess of Gloucester, with the Duke standing behind him.*

*With my stepfather in 1930, showing an early interest in cricket, and, I like to think, the beginnings of a half-decent cover drive! Helping to feed his polo ponies (BELOW, LEFT) and (BELOW, RIGHT) my sister Jonet, cutting a stylish dash on the beach during a family holiday.*

*My mother, with Jonet on her right, me on her left and my younger sister, Amanda, on her knee and (BELOW) with me again. Even then, the cricket bat was never far away.*

My mother was a friend of Lord and Lady Howard de Walden, who used to own the Isle of Shona, located in the Western Isles between Mull and Skye. We went to stay as holiday guests at their breath-takingly beautiful home, then the only house on the island (RIGHT). We would go by boat (ABOVE) for picnics on private beaches while I rowed out on fishing expeditions (BELOW) and caught my first mackerel.

*Clearly letting the tension get to me during a day at the races (ABOVE) and (LEFT) getting my hands on the trophy following another tournament victory for my step-father's polo team. That's him on the far left of the picture and (BELOW) mounted on a favourite pony.*

ABOVE: *My mother with her third husband, Mark Roddick, at a race meeting.*

RIGHT: *Me in full fig at Eton and* (BELOW) *sitting cross-legged in the front as a member of the cricket XI at St Aubyn's, my prep school in Sussex.*

LEFT: *A fleeting glimpse of me in uniform (centre) during my brief wartime army career. The shot was taken in Piccadilly Circus on VJ day in 1945. With me is my best friend at the time, Life Guard Jan Barnes, and a girlfriend of his.*

BELOW: *(looking into the camera) Me during my brief, dreadful spell as a 'Deb's Delight'!*

bring himself to speak to me, but informed me through a third party that although I had driven up with him from Calgary, he would not be able to give me a lift back. It then emerged that the four other English turncoats had also disowned me, promising him that they would not make room for me in their car. In the end, it was the Japanese wicket keeper who took pity on me and saved me the 400-mile walk back.

It was not long after this episode that I began to hanker once again for the green, green grass of home – and, in particular, the village cricket fields of Sussex.

V

# HALCYON DAYS

ERY FEW VILLAGE cricket clubs in England can claim to have a longer or more colourful history than Rottingdean C.C. The earliest documentary evidence of its existence comes in the form of an 18th-century poster that reads as follows:

"This is to acquaint the public that on Wednesday June 28th, 1758 will be played at Rottingdean, near Lewes, a great match of CRICKET for a Guinea a man. Newick, Chailey, Lindfield and Hamsey against Lewes, Brighthelmstone and Rottingdean. The wickets to be played at 12 o'clock and the game to be played out."

At around the same time, Rottingdean cricket was also celebrated in verse in an anonymous poem that includes the lines:

*Oh! See the matches on the Hill,*
*With the entire village keen,*
*Hark, how the air is ringing still*
*With cheers for Rottingdean!*

The original ground was situated up on Beacon Hill, near the windmill that still stands there to this day. The pitch itself faced out to sea, with the outfield sloping down towards the village on one side and towards Brighton on the other. Although the panoramic views from here were undoubtedly spectacular, the location was not entirely practical, as evidenced by several legendary incidents that are enshrined in local cricketing folklore

The most famous of these took place in around 1840 and resulted in what is claimed to be a world record for the number of runs scored off one ball. There were no boundaries in those days, so instead of hitting fours and sixes the batsmen had to run every run. On this occasion, a mighty strike sent the ball soaring so far over the outfield that when it did eventually come down to earth it caught the down slope and started bouncing faster and faster down the hillside towards the village, with the fielders stumbling in hot pursuit. It was eventually retrieved, but was so far from the wicket by this time that it had to be returned via a relay of fielders, while the batsmen continued to run.

The inevitable then happened. The batsmen had already run thirty-eight by now and, whether because they were too greedy or simply because they had lost concentration and hadn't noticed that the ball was now in the hands of a close-in fielder, they set off for a very risky thirty-ninth. In his excitement at the prospect of a run-out, the fielder tried to throw down the wicket, but hurled the ball so hard and so wide of the mark that it disappeared down the hill on the other side with the result that the whole process had to be repeated.

The exhausted batsmen eventually ran sixty-eight. At twenty-two yards per run, that works out at a total of 1,496 yards – very nearly a mile. Given that they were wearing pads, carrying a bat and were very likely further encumbered by a dislodged box, I can only surmise that they were a jolly sight fitter than I ever was, even at the peak of my playing career! It makes me feel quite faint to think about it.

Another story from around this time involves a batsman who, facing out to sea and about to receive a ball, suddenly stepped away from the crease as the bowler was about to deliver and held up his hand to indicate that he wasn't quite ready.

A polite version of the exchange that is said to have followed would probably have been along the lines of:

Bowler (Observing the usual courtesies extended to batsmen at such moments!): "I say, old chap, whatever could it be that is bothering you? Do please take your time to get comfortable and then perhaps I may be allowed to proceed."

Batsman (Equally polite, as we always are in the South of England): "I'm awfully sorry to be such a terrible nuisance, but there is a sailing ship passing on the horizon behind your bowling arm and it's putting me off somewhat."

Play was then allegedly suspended for twenty minutes.

This may possibly be apocryphal, but the equally colourful explanation for why the location of the ground was eventually moved in 1880 from Beacon Hill to its present position just outside the village down below has never been disputed.

The heavy roller that was used on the pitch weighed nearly a ton and it took several members of the team to operate it, one lot pulling from the front while others pushed from behind. Exactly what caused the mishap is not known – maybe just over-enthusiasm or perhaps a bit of horseplay – but one weekend, as they were hauling it off the square, they somehow lost control and it started rolling down the hill towards the village.

There was no chance of stopping it once it started gathering pace and they could only look on in horror and bellow warnings to anyone who might be in its path as it careered and rumbled some two hundred yards down the hill, scattering startled sheep on the way. Fortunately, there were no courting couples lurking in the long grass, as was so often the case in high summer!

Miraculously, the roller eventually came to rest without causing any major damage apart from smashing through a fence and flattening part of a hedge. If it had had two fingers, it might have raised them to the shocked players gazing down, as if to indicate that it had wanted to get out of that bloody east wind up there for years and now it was happy.

Just about every able-bodied man in the village was mobilised in an effort to pull it back up the hill, but without the slightest success. It wouldn't budge. The next day they tried with a couple of carthorses, again to no avail. The iron monster did not want to co-operate.

The farmer who owned the field where the roller was now

stranded, and who happened to be an enthusiastic member of the club, then made the very logical suggestion that perhaps the mountain should come to Mohammed and that the ground should be moved to the field to accommodate the runaway roller. He was immediately made club president as a mark of gratitude for his lateral thinking and for the use of his land. The field was mown, a wicket prepared, a pavilion built and the club settled into this new and even more attractive setting, where it has been ever since.

In 2008, Rottingdean C.C. will celebrate its 250th anniversary and I am very proud to have played a small part in its long history, as player, captain, Hon. Sec. and president at various times during my active 37-year association with the club.

I first became involved, quite by chance, in 1948. My mother had grown up in that part of the world, her family home being near Lewes, and before I went to Eton I was sent to St Aubyn's – or 'Stubbins' as Old Boys tend to call it – a preparatory school in Rottingdean. One of the masters there was a marvellous chap called 'Pop' Coates, a giant of a man who stood about six-foot-four and had been a very handy bowler in his day. He was the sports master in charge of cricket and, as such, was the one who first got me interested in the game. Just after the war, at around the time that I was living in Walton Street, I bumped into him again in a pub one day. We got chatting and he invited me to come down and turn out for Rottingdean.

He explained to me that the club had virtually ceased to exist during the war, its ground having been commandeered by the military as a park for armoured vehicles. As a result, the playing area had been badly churned up and covered in rubble and concrete in parts to provide hard standings, while the old wooden pavilion had fallen into a state of near dereliction. With no ground, no playing members and no fixtures, the club organisation had simply collapsed and disintegrated.

It was another master at St Aubyn's, Eric Webber, who came to the rescue, helped by his wife, Barbie, and Henry Blyth, the author and scriptwriter who, along with Jack Davies, co-wrote the scripts for most of the Norman Wisdom films. Between them, these three revived the club and gave it a new lease of life during the forties, fifties and sixties, when traditional village cricket was still enjoying a golden age.

Eric, who went on to become joint headmaster at St Aubyn's, was a wonderful though occasionally rather eccentric character. As well as his passion for cricket, he was a horse racing addict and a do-it-yourself enthusiast. He also had an eye for any attractive lady. Indeed, my sister Jonet once had to hurl herself out of a ground floor bedroom window and into a flowerbed to escape his advances!

Barbie was an equally colourful character, with a very strong personality. She was extremely energetic and an absolute whizz at any kind of organisation. She ended up doing everything from acting as club secretary – taking and typing up all the minutes, confirming fixtures and looking after all the rest of the administration – right through to finding volunteer tea ladies on match days, and then making all the sandwiches herself.

Henry was a very keen sportsman and a former Half Blue at Oxford. Next to cricket his dearest love was his Rolls Royce, from which all of us in the team without transport of our own managed to benefit from time to time, rolling up to away matches in some style.

I should mention at this point that the only car I have ever owned in my life was a 1939 3½-litre Lagonda Coupe that I bought from a dealer in Hammersmith just after the war for £400. I had it for about four months before it broke down and was found to have sawdust in the gearbox, or whatever it was that shady second-hand car dealers used to do to make clapped out cars drive OK for a few hundred miles before giving up the ghost amid a cloud of smoke and a trail of leaking oil. I sold it on at a considerable loss and have never felt the need to own another car since then. Many years later, I saw the exact same Lagonda, by then a sought-after classic, advertised for sale at £20,000!

By the time that 'Pop' Coates invited me down to play in the summer of 1948, Eric, Barbie and Henry had already got the club up and running again. The ground had been cleared and put back in order, the wicket itself had been lovingly restored with much mowing, rolling and scarifying, the dilapidated pavilion had been renovated and an attractive fixture list had been re-established with all the old local rivals from neighbouring villages around Sussex.

Apart from 1953/4, when I was in Canada, I was a regular member of the team for the next twenty-two years, eventually taking over as captain and Hon. Sec. and then later, when my playing days were over, going on to become president for ten years in the seventies and eighties. From 1948-70 I spent virtually every weekend during the season in Sussex, travelling down from London by train after work on Friday evenings to stay with the Webbers at their home in Southerndown, where they were kind enough to put a room aside for me. I would then return on Monday mornings on the Brighton Belle. Not surprisingly, Eric and Barbie, along with their lovely daughters, Toni and Stephanie, became like a second family for me.

This was undoubtedly one of the happiest periods of my entire life, what I always look back on as my halcyon days. My abiding memories are of long, hot summer afternoons spent playing on some of the loveliest village grounds and amid some of the most glorious countryside to be found anywhere in England; of close-fought matches played in a marvellous spirit of camaraderie and of fun and games on and off the pitch. I made many great friends and had some wonderful times.

At the same time, I also found my true calling at last when I landed a job as an advertising executive with fledgling commercial television station Southern TV. Before that, there had been several other false starts immediately following my return from Canada. A spell in the advertising department of the *London Evening News* lasted only a few months, largely because of a personality clash with my boss, who clearly despised my Old Etonian background.

Next came a job as sales manager of the Ellern Paper Company. This sounds a lot better than it actually was, since the paper in question was actually lavatory paper. Hans Ellern was an Austrian Jew, who had escaped over the mountains in 1939 and came to England where he set up his business supplying Boots and Woolworths with their own-brand products.

Hans was very ambitious, determined to become the leader in his chosen field and to wipe the floor, as it were, with the competition. To this end, he decided that he would be the first to launch coloured loo paper in the UK. It was to spearhead this campaign that I was hired, with orders to build up a sales force of four to promote OZO.

This was never going to be an easy assignment, for at least three very good reasons: firstly, Bowater Scott (Andrex) and Kimberley Clark (Delsey), our main competitors, were known to be launching their own coloured brands in the near future; secondly, our advertising budget of £10,000 was a tenth of what they were each planning to spend; and thirdly, I had virtually no experience.

Hans, dominating and belligerent, was undeterred by all this. A launch date was set and an agency briefed to produce an advertising campaign. Given that one half-page ad in the *Evening Standard* alone cost £5,000 – half our entire planned budget – this was not very extensive.

The agency duly came up with a proposal for a very simple ad that was to feature an attractive blonde holding up the various coloured rolls with the message: "It's Blue. It's Green. It's Yellow. It's Peachy!" At this point, I then had the bright idea of saving the cost of hiring a professional model to pose for the ad by using, instead, a girlfriend of mine who had ambitions to become a model herself and was happy to do it for nothing. This was fine except that I had overlooked the fact that her father happened to be a Lord Lieutenant. He and his family were far from delighted to see their daughter plastered all over the *Evening Standard* holding up rolls of lavatory paper.

This was not the only way in which the job was undermining my social standing. I was in danger of becoming obsessed with the product, albeit, I thought, in a rather witty and amusing way. The sad truth, of course, is that lavatory paper is a bit of a turn-off as a subject for cocktail party small talk. At one such do I made the terrible mistake of light-heartedly presenting my hostess with a free sample, along with what was intended as a hilarious, tongue-in-cheek spiel about its superior softness and aesthetic appeal. After that I noticed that the invitations were suddenly starting to dry up.

I was saved from further embarrassment when the inevitable happened and the OZO brand went down the pan, though not quite in the way that Hans had envisaged. As Andrex and Delsey cleaned up, his dreams of market domination collapsed and not long after that my job went too. That turned out to be a blessing in disguise since it was the catalyst that led me, in 1958, to join Southern TV. From then on I never really looked back.

While my exciting new career provided me with real job satisfaction for the first time, cricket remained my great passion. I am aware that 'boring old farts' like myself are always harping back to better days, but I do believe that club cricket in those post-war years before the leagues came in was very, very special. Things were never quite the same again after they introduced the league system in the seventies. League cricket had been played in the North very successfully for years and Northerners could never quite understand how Southerners were able to enjoy playing each other purely for pleasure, rather than for points. In fact, we had always played just as hard, but as soon as points came into it there was a different attitude. People would do anything to avoid losing and the fun started to go out of it. Also, a lot of the old traditional fixtures went out of the window because sides that had been playing each other for years suddenly found that they were in different divisions. One way and another, I'm rather glad that my regular playing career ended when it did and I feel very fortunate that it coincided with the amateur game's golden era.

It has to be admitted that one of the other factors contributing to the decline of that golden era was the advent of the breathalyser. This had a sobering effect on the traditional post-match celebrations in the home team's local pub that had always been such an important part of the whole ritual of village cricket. These sessions would often last long into the night and the journey home could not always be remembered too clearly the next morning. Obviously, there is no way that one could possibly defend that sort of behaviour, but the new culture of having just a quick pint of shandy after the game before going home did not encourage the sort of socialising and all-round banter and bonhomie without which a large part of the enjoyment went missing.

As an example of how things used to be in the good old, bad old days, let me recall the events one particular August Bank Holiday in the fifties.

I had been invited to turn out for a club called The Brighton Brunswick, based at the Sussex county ground at Hove. The captain at the time was Norman Wilson, whose family had contributed an enormous amount to cricket in Sussex, and it was a great honour to be invited to play for them.

The fixture on this occasion was away to Reading, a very strong club side whose captain happened to be the landlord of a riverside pub, conveniently located not very far from their ground.

It was a glorious, sunny summer's day, I remember. The match started at 11.30am and finished at 7.00pm. It was a great game. The result was immaterial to the events that followed, but I think we lost.

After the match, both sides retired to the skipper's pub. At around 9.30pm, by which time things were starting to go with a real swing, the landlord suddenly expressed profound apologies for having clean forgotten to arrange something he had been meaning to do all along. He then proceeded to ring Reading General Hospital and could be overheard telling someone on the other end of the line that as many nurses as possible were urgently required at the pub. We thought this a good gag and continued our drinking. To our astonishment, ten nurses duly appeared about thirty minutes later, and another happy hour passed.

At 10.30pm the landlord then announced that he was terribly sorry but we would have to call it a day, otherwise he would be in danger of losing his licence. He added, however, that there was a private party going on at the pub on the other side of the river, immediately opposite, and that he was sure we would be welcome there.

We needed no further encouragement and went down to the riverside to assess the situation and to find some means of getting across. At this point we spotted a rowing boat moored alongside a private jetty and decided to commandeer it without further ado. Surely it wouldn't be missed for an hour or so?

Ten of us, plus one nurse, then piled into the small boat, navigated our way rather uncertainly across the river and, on landing, proceeded to the place from which music and lots of jolly laughter was emanating. And so it was that the members of the Reading Ladies Bowling Club were suddenly confronted at their annual dinner dance by a gaggle of ten, very well-oiled cricketers and one slightly squiffy nurse. They were not amused and, at their suggestion, we left immediately and retreated back to 'our' boat.

I should explain that we were all in different forms of attire, some in suits, some in casual gear and myself still in white flannels and cricket boots. I was the first to jump into the boat. I sat down in the front, facing the other bank, whilst the others, including the nurse, piled in behind and somebody grabbed an oar. As we then pursued an even more erratic course back towards the other side, I began to feel somewhat damp, a sensation that increased with each wild stroke of the oar. Turning around to ascertain what the problem was, I quickly realised that we were sinking. It transpired that when I had jumped in I had put my foot through a plank, causing our predicament.

What I saw as I turned round were nine chaps (and one nurse) talking to each other in animated fashion, apparently oblivious to the fact that the water level in the boat was now rapidly rising towards their waists.

In fact, one bloke was in the act of saying: "Sorry, Fred, I can't play next week because ...", at which point he and the rest of us subsided gracefully beneath the surface. One of our number, a wonderful eighteen stoner, nearly succumbed because every time he came to the surface he bellowed with hilarious laughter before sinking out of sight again. On the third occasion, the rest of us had to struggle to hold him up.

We eventually clambered ashore to be greeted by two police cars, four policemen and one hysterical lady boat owner. We were all lined up while the police attempted to take names and addresses. I came off worst since three of my colleagues had already given my name. When the policeman came to me, he warned: "Now, don't you start by telling me you are Tony Salisbury!"

We did eventually manage to resolve the situation amicably by collecting a sufficient amount of cash to placate the lady boat owner, who, very sportingly, did not prefer charges.

Even then, the evening's entertainment was not finished. Most of the team, still in wet clothing, poured themselves into their cars and set off for Brighton. Our skipper, Norman Wilson, who had come up the previous day and had stayed overnight, decided that he would first change from his sodden clothes into his pyjamas before driving home.

Thus clad, and having experienced slight difficulty in finding his way out of Reading, he was stopped at 2.30am by two slightly incredulous policemen.

"Would you mind pulling over to the kerb, Sir, so that we can have a little chat." Norman did as requested.

"Now, Sir", continued the copper, "I wonder if would mind explaining to us why you are driving around in a motor vehicle at 2.30am, wearing your pyjamas?"

Without hesitation, Norman replied: "Well, you see, officer, I am inclined to go to sleep at the wheel."

Game, set and match to Norman. He was given directions and allowed to drive on. But just imagine the trouble he would be in today in similar circumstances!

One of my earliest Rottingdean memories concerns a match in 1951 against arch rivals Henfield when it was over-indulgence before the game that was my downfall. On this occasion, the Webbers, with whom I was already in the habit of staying at weekends, had been invited by the Captain of the Ark Royal for pre-lunch drinks aboard an aircraft carrier that was anchored just off Brighton Pier as part of a goodwill visit and I was taken along too.

The match with Henfield was due to start at 2.00pm that after-noon and I thought that a taxi at 1.15pm would get me there in plenty of time. However, as the Martinis and pink gins slipped down, I missed the announcement that the lighter taking members of the general public back to shore was about to depart. It then emerged that the one taking special guests such as the Webbers and myself would not be leaving until 2.00pm, much too late for me.

"No problem," said the Captain when I explained my predica-ment. "You can go on the Captain's barge, which is leaving in ten minutes with the ship's cricket XI, who happen to be playing in Brighton."

A senior aide, who had been detailed by the Captain to conduct me to the barge, pointed over the rail to a deck below and told me to get on board. I climbed down and arrived by the side of the waiting barge. "Excuse me," I said to a young Officer. "I've been told you can kindly take me ashore."

"I think not," he said, rather snootily "This is for Ark Royal crew only."

I looked up to the higher deck where the aide was looking down at us.

"Er, I say, Sir," I shouted. "This chap won't let me on board."

"Lieutenant Richardson," bellowed the Aide. "This fellow is a guest of the Captain, so I suggest you let him on board immediately."

The twelve others on board eyed me with suspicion and you could cut the atmosphere with the proverbial knife. I scrambled on board in deathly silence and went to sit at the stern, near the propeller. We then started the comparatively short journey only for the engine to conk out halfway across, leaving us drifting helplessly. As part of this big naval occasion, there were two Canadian destroyers moored nearby and the unpleasant, sulky and now highly embarrassed young Lieutenant ordered that we make for the nearest of these two ships. After a lot of tinkering, the barge was restarted, but for some reason could only be driven backwards. As I was sitting next to the propeller, this meant that a sizeable amount of the English Channel landed in my lap. By the time we reached the destroyer my inside was awash with martinis and my outside with gallons of seawater.

We clambered aboard and were welcomed by the Canadian Captain, who said he would arrange to have us taken ashore in about half an hour. In the meantime, he hoped that we would join him in the wardroom for drinks. My heart sank. It was already after 2.00pm and my match would already be underway. I had my cricket bag with me and decided to change out of my wet clothes into my cricket gear, much to the further annoyance of the sulky Lieutenant.

A number of pink gins later and we were once more on our way. I managed to find a taxi and eventually arrived at Henfield at 4.00pm. As I prepared to go out and join my team-mates on the field, I heard rumbles from the opposition, who seemed to think that my late arrival was all part of a devious plan aimed at ensuring that, without much fielding, I would be kept fresh for batting!

Considering that I was full of at least five martinis and four large pink gins, that didn't hold much water.

Needless to say, I was out very quickly, despite my advance billing as our side's star batsman, and we went on to lose ignominiously. I was not very popular. And to make matters worse, I couldn't even face the thought of more booze in the pub afterwards with which to drown my sorrows.

Among our regular opponents, Cuckfield, Ditchling, Findon, Scaynes Hill and Roffey were all lovely villages with wonderful cricket grounds and many legendary characters among their players. However, our rivalry with Henfield was particularly intense.

Both clubs were jealous of each other's historical past. Rottingdean always considered themselves the older club, their first recorded match dating back to 1758, but then Henfield put it about that whilst ploughing a field adjacent to their ground a local farmer had unearthed documents that appeared to record a game some years earlier than ours! This only served to intensify the antagonism.

Every match was a needle match, eagerly looked forward to by both sides. Henfield's ground and pavilion was truly perfect and really picturesque, with an excellent wicket. They also had a very large contingent of the most partisan supporters I have ever played against, some of whom were quite prepared to resort to any tricks in an effort to influence the result.

I recall one occasion when Henfield were batting and heading towards a very modest total, with only a few tail-end batsmen left. I was fielding on the square leg boundary, which was protected by some low wooden fencing behind which were seated a few hundred apparently respectable spectators. The batsman hooked a long hop and sent it soaring high in the air towards the boundary some distance to my right. I started sprinting round the boundary in the hope of pulling off a spectacular catch. As the ball then started to drop it was clear that instead of going for six it was going to fall just inside the boundary. I was going flat out, keeping my eye fixed firmly on the ball and was almost underneath it, my hands outstretched to take the catch, when I suddenly tripped over something and fell flat on my face. One of the spectators had stuck an umbrella out from the boundary fence!

On another occasion one of our fielders was perfectly positioned on the boundary as a similar high shot was hit in his direction. As the ball reached its zenith and started to drop into his waiting hands he suddenly noticed that it was no longer alone. There were three of them! He panicked, let out a cry and, cowering on his haunches, covered his head with his hands. Whereupon a cricket ball and two oranges rained down on him!

Henfield has had many fine cricketers in its time, including C. Aubrey Smith, who was their captain before going on to play for Sussex and England. Trevor Adcock might well have emulated that feat had he not been mysteriously overlooked when he went for a county trial with Sussex, despite his obvious promise as a youngster. He was certainly the best batsman of my generation in Sussex club cricket, followed closely by my great friend, Peter Beecheno. Trevor was way above everybody else's standard, once scoring 185 out of his side's total of 220.

He was a terribly nice chap and although fierce rivals on the field we were also good mates. And together we became involved in one of the more remarkable incidents in the history of Rottingdean's encounters with Henfield.

We were playing at Henfield in 1967. I was captain at the time and, as so often, was finding it impossible to do anything to stop the flow of runs from Trevor's bat. However much I changed the bowling or altered the field, nothing seemed to work and he was making his usual rapid progress towards another century.

He arrived at 99 and I decided to gamble with an appeal to his love of a challenge. "OK Trevor," I said as the field changed at the end of the over. "I know you would like to get your ton with a six, so I'm going to put on a slow spinner. It's all set up for you – but I'm going to be fielding on the long-on boundary, down by the sightscreen, ready to catch you if you get it wrong." He grinned at me and awaited the start of the over.

Jimmy Gould bowled him a good length ball. Trevor stepped forward and hit it nicely on the up, high and hard and straight down the wicket. It was definitely going for six over the fence down by the sightscreen, except that this was exactly where I had positioned myself. I didn't have to move, just stretched out an arm and managed to hold on to the ball as it was about to sail over the fence. Trevor hadn't hit it quite well enough. He grinned, raised his bat and left.

When it came to our turn to bat, we were chasing 260. I went in at No.3, as usual, and enjoyed one of my better days. After a flurry of fours and sixes I, too, found myself on 99.

Trevor was fielding at cover. The bowler went back to his mark. Trevor's voice came to me from the covers. "Here I am, Tony," he shouted, beaming broadly and cupping his hands in front of him in an exaggerated fashion.

"Don't be so bloody silly" I retorted and proceeded to miss-hit the next ball straight into his hands.

The highest score I ever made was 120. That was against Newhaven, on the least attractive of all the grounds we ever played on, a bleak, windy field with old wartime pillbox defences all over the place. Because of that, the innings was never that memorable for me. The real highpoint of my cricketing career was in 1962 when I became the first batsman in the history of Rottingdean ever to score 1,000 runs in a season.

The slightly controversial manner in which this feat was achieved has since been written about in two books, *The Clouds Are High* and *The Domestic Cricketer*, and the story has also been recounted in numerous club bars and pubs over the years. However, certain aspects have been grossly exaggerated. In particular, it is not quite true that in order to reach the 1,000-run mark I had to arrange ten additional matches, extending the scheduled end of the season well into December.

What actually happened was that on September 30th I walked to the crease for the last match of the season having scored a grand total of 980 runs. Unfortunately, I then made only 6, leaving me fourteen short of the magic 1,000.

We happened to playing against St. James, whose team included one of my closest friends, Peter Beecheno. As already mentioned, Peter was one of the best club bowlers and batsmen in Southern England. He was also a most astute captain, with an exceptional ability to remember opposing players' individual weaknesses.

When I had gone in to bat in the previous year's encounter, with Peter bowling, I had, as usual, taken my guard, made my mark and then looked up to check the field placings. To my astonishment, I saw that the leg-side was devoid of fielders. All nine, apart from Peter and the wicket keeper, were on the off-side – a mid off, a deep mid off, a deep, deep mid off, a cover, extra cover, deep extra cover, deep point and two slips. I looked down the wicket at Peter, who stood there grinning broadly as he slowly raised two fingers.

Well that did it! I hit his first ball clean over the sightscreen and returned the gesture. I tried to do the same with the next ball and slightly miscued, whereupon three mid offs and two covers all shouted "Mine!" and I returned to the pavilion.

Back to the last match of the 1962 season. In The Plough afterwards, as we were drinking our pints by the pond on a lovely autumn evening, everyone began to commiserate about my narrow failure to reach the 1,000 mark.

Peter suddenly looked up at the sky thoughtfully and murmured: "The clouds are high and the weather looks set fair for at least a week, so why not have another match next Saturday?" Everyone agreed and we decided we would be able to play until 6.00pm before the light faded.

We played. I went in to bat. I scored 4. Still short.

We retired to the pub. Further commiserations. Another match was arranged.

We played. I scored 6. Four short.

Back at the pub, enthusiasm was starting to wane. The days were drawing in and the clocks were about to go back. If there was to be yet another match we would have to start at 11.30am in order to get finished before dark.

For his part, the landlord of The Plough agreed to open the back door early, at 4.45pm, which was not going to be a problem because the village bobby was a member of the Rottingdean side!

The weather still held, but it was decidedly chilly. I scored only 3. 1 run short!

We were now into November. Twenty-one players were becoming increasingly cheesed off and all sympathy was quickly evaporating. My pleas for one more chance were only very reluctantly accepted after I offered to buy several gallons of beer. A final match was arranged for the following week, November 7th.

I understand that at this point I was very nearly responsible for a divorce. When one of the team was observed trying to sneak out of the house at 10.30am with his cricket bag, his wife inquired suspiciously: "And where do you think you are going?"

"To play cricket, of course," he replied defensively. "That is why I'm carrying a cricket bag."

"You really expect me to believe that?" snorted his wife. "I may not know a lot about cricket, but I do know that it's a summer game and we're now well into the football season. So, come on. Who is she?"

It was only when he suggested that she might like to come along as a spectator that she accepted he might be telling the truth.

People trooped out onto the field wearing about three sweaters. Nobody was very enthusiastic. We were all bloody cold. Everyone was desperate for me to score the one run so that we could get the game over with as soon as possible and then go and have drink.

Missing one regular member of their team, the opposition had had to ring around at the last moment to find a replacement. He was unaware of the reason for this strangely un-seasonal match, but was lured by the promise of free beer.

It came to my turn to bat and the inevitable happened. I hit the ball high into the off side of the field where their substitute fielder stood, hands cupped, waiting to take this dolly drop catch.

At this point at least five fielders cried out in unison: "For ****'s sake, drop the ****** thing!"

He was so startled that he did just that.

And that, I swear, is the truth about how I became the first and only Rottingdean batsman in the club's 250-year history to score 1,000 runs in a season. I consider it a gross slander to suggest that it required ten extra matches and that the last one was played with only five shopping days to go to Christmas and a light covering of snow on the outfield!

# VI

## TV TIMES

COMMERCIAL TELEVISION as a whole was still in its infancy when, in 1958, Southern Television became the sixth regional ITV company to go on air, having won the franchise for Central Southern England.

It was all very new and exciting territory to most of those involved in the company and many of us found ourselves on a very steep learning curve. This was especially true of the Advertising Sales Department, a very mixed bag of characters, with varying degrees of experience in selling, very little in advertising and, of course, none at all in television.

In the months leading up to the launch in August 1958, we spent most of our time rushing around making our presence known to the advertising industry in general and, in particular, to the main advertising agencies and major manufacturers such as Unilever and Procter & Gamble.

Our first office consisted of little more than a collection of soap boxes and three telephones in a pokey little room in Television House, Holborn. We then moved into more spacious premises just down the road in Brettenham House, which was located on the corner of Waterloo Bridge, conveniently adjacent to the Savoy.

Here, we all worked in a large open plan office where the noise was tremendous, the working hours lengthy and the lunches extended. We did a huge amount of entertaining, this being the surest way to develop immediate and long-term associations with our customers. At the same time, we were also having to develop relationships with one another from scratch, since we had all been rather suddenly and haphazardly thrown together, having come from very different walks of life and social classes. As it happens, I think this wide variety of backgrounds was probably one of the secrets of our success.

A sense of humour (occasionally rather black!) and an interest in sport were important factors in the 'bonding' process. One of the early victims of the boisterous prankishness that often prevailed was a chap named Mick, who could only cope efficiently with clients if he conducted telephone conversations from a position under his desk. He couldn't concentrate otherwise because of all the noise and general mayhem around him.

A plan was soon hatched to take advantage of this idiosyncrasy. Peter, a very good mimic, telephoned him from the other end of the room and, with a heavy Scottish accent, introduced himself as the Managing Director of a company that had invented a special new kind of children's drinking straw. These straws, he explained, were unique in that they were edible and came in a range of flavours – orange, raspberry and so on. (Not a bad idea at all, come to think of it!) He went on to say that he would like to arrange an urgent meeting in his Aberdeen office to discuss a possible schedule for test marketing on Southern TV.

We had all watched as Mick dived under his desk to take the call and were now monitoring the proceedings with varying degrees of scarcely suppressed glee.

"What is the size of your universe?" growled Peter down the phone – 'universe' being adspeak for the number of viewers one could claim to reach. Mick's head popped up from under the desk. "I say, chaps, anybody know what our universe is?" he shouted.

"180,000," we yelled back.

He disappeared under the desk again to impart this information.

"Excellent," said Peter. "In that case I would like a meeting in my office at ten o'clock tomorrow morning to discuss the details. Can you make it up here by then?"

"Hold on," said Mick, increasingly excited at the prospect of landing a lucrative account. His face reappeared. "Anyone got a timetable of night trains to Aberdeen?" he called out.

We were already prepared for this. "There's one out of Euston at 11.00pm," someone shouted in reply. "Arrives Aberdeen at 7.30am."

Back under the desk, with the phone clamped to one ear and a finger stuck in the other, Mick could be heard saying: "No problem. There's a sleeper that gets in at 7.30am. Could I have your address, please?"

"Allsop Works, Stonehill Road," Peter told him. "Any taxi driver will know where we are. See you tomorrow."

Mick re-emerged with a smile of triumph on his face, convinced that the deal was as good as in the bag. To our eternal shame, we let him go. On his return, he was in a very peculiar mood for quite a few weeks.

Another joke that went a bit too far, with much more serious repercussions, involved one of the two lift attendants at Brettenham House. As a result of an accident suffered many years before, this poor fellow had a wooden leg of which he was inordinately proud. He used to joke that it never gave him any pain when he barked his shins. One day, as a bunch of us were returning from an enjoyable lunch with a new colleague who had only just joined us in the office, we told him about the leg and said that the attendant would consider it an amusing joke if he were to give it a playful kick, accompanied by a light-hearted comment along the lines of: "Just testing, mate."

The newcomer thought this was a splendid idea and as we all entered the lift he lashed out and delivered a thumping great kick to the man's leg. Unfortunately, he had not only chosen the wrong leg, but the wrong man. This resulted in a visit to casualty and then developed into a serious Union matter, eventually necessitating delicate negotiations between the Managing Director, Union officials and the owners of the building. In the end, things were only resolved with the payment of a fairly hefty sum in damages.

During all these pre-launch shenanigans, we were working at an increasingly hectic pace to maximise our advertising revenue from the on-air date of August 28th.

We knew that the South of England was an exceptionally valuable and important area for advertisers, not only because of its comparative wealth of population, but also because in many ways the buying habits of Southerners, generally, were very similar to those of Londoners. This enabled us to gain an additional revenue advantage over the rest of the country through being used as a 'test' area for new products before they were launched in the greater and considerably more expensive London region.

However, when we issued our first rate card, showing the rates charged for the various advertising slots available, we made the mistake of omitting to offer a 'development' discount for the first six months, as all the other major television regions before us had done. This was a bad error of judgement, but even worse was the manner in which we went about presenting our rate card to the major television advertiser at that time, the soap and detergent manufacturer Procter & Gamble.

A golden rule for any salesman is that he must always remember to do his homework on the potential client – and that means not just the company, but also the senior executive with whom he is likely to be dealing. Procter & Gamble's marketing boss was not only very tough and very powerful, with very little sense of humour, but was also a Quaker to boot! My boss, John Miell, a wonderfully extrovert character, had failed to take this fully on board. And in his usual uninhibited creative style, he decided to present our rate card to this gentleman over dinner in London's famous West End night club, the Pigalle.

The club's cabaret famously featured numerous very scantily-clad dancing girls and was in every possible way a totally inappropriate venue for a teetotal, non-smoking Quaker. But John's misjudgement did not end there. He had gone to great lengths to make an arrangement with the management whereby a waitress dressed in a bunny girl outfit would arrive at the table and, rather than presenting his guest with a menu, would hand him instead the Southern Television rate card! It took weeks, not to mention the introduction of a handsome 'development discount', to atone for this double blunder.

John Miell was not the only one who unwittingly fell foul of this particular executive's puritanical tastes. The sales director of another ITV company was guilty of an even greater howler when he took it upon himself to arrange overnight accommodation for him after he had announced his intention of coming down to visit the company at their London office. The company chairman had a permanent suite at the Dorchester Hotel and told the Sales Director to offer it to this VIP client for the night in question. The offer was gratefully accepted and on the day in question the Procter & Gamble man presented himself at the reception desk.

Welcome Sir", beamed the receptionist. "The suite is at your disposal. Would you mind just signing the book?" He duly did so. "Thank you, Sir, but would you mind signing your wife in as well."

"That won't be necessary," he replied. "My wife is not with me on this occasion."

"I quite understand, Sir," said the receptionist with a knowing smile. "But I do need you to sign her in."

"I just told you, my wife is not with me," he snapped angrily.

"I know, Sir, but could you please just sign her in anyway," pleaded the receptionist.

At this point the penny dropped. Furiously, the Procter & Gamble man stormed up to the suite, phoned his advertising agency and instructed them to cancel all television advertising with the company forthwith. At the time, that probably accounted for 15% of their total advertising revenue. All hell then broke loose and the crisis was only resolved when the Chairman, personally, went to Newcastle to apologise profusely for such scandalous behaviour on the part of his Sales Director. In the Sales Director's defence, I have to say that the provision of a high-class call girl for an important client was not unusual and would have been gratefully accepted by nearly anyone else other than a Quaker.

In these early days of ITV commercials before the advent of videotape, commercials were either supplied on film or as still slides with a voice-over and were sometimes even broadcast 'live' from the TV studios. Among the consortium that owned Southern Television were Associated Newspapers, owners of *The Daily Mail*. They were one of our main advertisers and at one point I suggested the idea of a nightly 'live' commercial, highlighting the lead stories that would be appearing in the *Mail* the following day.

It was agreed they would give it a five-day trail. The plan was that a two-minute commercial would be transmitted at 10.40pm each night from the Southampton studios. I would attend the *Daily Mail* newsroom each evening and telephone summaries of the three main stories to our studio half an hour before transmission. The presenter would then run through them on air.

This all seemed fairly simple and straightforward and, for me personally, rather exciting. Apart from anything else, it gave me the opportunity to work with Arthur Brittenden, the paper's night editor and, later, its editor, a most charming and delightful man whom I have since come to count amongst my closest and dearest friends. However, as I have so often found to my cost, simple, straightforward plans have a habit of becoming unexpectedly complicated – so disastrously so in this particular instance as to seriously jeopardise our license to broadcast.

I should explain that our overall masters at the time were the Independent Television Authority, who appointed the broadcasting companies and imposed a whole range of strict rules and regulations in regard to the transmission of programmes and commercials. These were policed through the Advertising Control department. All scripts, storyboards and completed commercials had to be approved in advance, to ensure that the public were not misled by false claims or subjected to unacceptable sexual overtones or violence.

The head of Advertising Control was a wonderful Scotsman called Archie Graham. Archie was liked and respected by all the television companies, agencies and advertisers, despite the fact that he was tough as old boots – famed for playing golf in shorts at all times of the year, whatever the weather. He didn't miss a trick and very few of us got away with anything while Archie was in control.

The first day at the *Daily Mail* newsroom was to be a dry run, which hopefully would sort out the procedures and the linkage between me and the studio.

I had also been carefully briefed by Archie Graham as to my responsibilities for the clearance of the copy, which could not be vetted by the Clearance Committee in the usual way as it was going out live. I was given the home telephone numbers of Archie and two other members of the Committee in the event I needed guidance.

I had everything under complete control, a production system in place and my masters available in the wings. The blame for what was to follow I attribute entirely to Arthur Brittenden's over-generous hospitality.

On my arrival that first evening at 7.00pm, he greeted me warmly, invited me into his office and placed a bottle of whisky in front of me. "Help yourself," he said airily. "I'm going to be rushing around for the next couple of hours and then I will probably be able to give you an idea of our main lead stories for tomorrow".

I poured myself a large measure and sat back to watch all the feverish activity of the paper being put to bed. Now that computer technology has replaced hot metal printing, a relatively subdued silence has fallen over newsrooms that once used to echo to the clatter of typewriters and the shouts of sub-editors calling for copy boys to collect the edited copy and rush it to the linotype operators. As a result, some of the drama has now gone out of the countdown to the deadlines for the first edition of a national newspaper, but back then you could hear, see and feel the tension mounting all around you. I expected someone to rush in at any moment, shouting: "Hold the front page!" With so much going on, time passed quickly – and so did the Scotch!

Arthur then suddenly reappeared, in a state of some considerable excitement.

"We have the lead story for tomorrow and it's a major scoop," he said. "We've managed to sign up Greville Wynn, the spy captured by the Russians and released by them today. He is giving us his exclusive story".

This was something really special and, fortified by a considerable amount of whisky, I made an instant executive decision.

"Right" I said. "There'll be no dry run tonight. We'll go live in ninety minutes".

I telephoned our studios in Southampton and spoke to the producer.

"We're going live, George," I announced dramatically. "I'll clear the commercial break of advertisements, brief the presenter and be back with the script in one hour".

I contacted the commercial transmission department and told them to clear out the scheduled commercial in the two-minute break at 10.40.

"OK," I was told. "But you realise there is a 60-second commercial for Persil in there?"

"That's alright," I said boldly. "I'll deal with the Unilever agency tomorrow morning".

Apart from Procter & Gamble, Unilever was our major client and it was only much later, when the euphoria and the whisky had worn off, that I realised I would undoubtedly have a problem on my hands, trying to placate what was certain to be a very angry client.

Meanwhile, everything had been finalised. The three lead stories had been scripted and phoned down to Southampton and the two-minute commercial was successfully transmitted without any hitches. I went to bed a contented and happy man and was back in my office the next morning full of beans, expecting to bask in the warm congratulations of colleagues impressed by how clever and quick-thinking I had been.

My phone rang. It was an angry Unilever man demanding to know what had happened to his Persil ad. I managed to placate him by discounting the price of some future transmissions. The phone rang again.

It was the Head of Advertising Control, Archie Graham. He did not sound at all happy, either.

"You are in trouble, laddie," he said in his heavy Scottish accent. "What's more, your company is in trouble. And, most important, I am in trouble with the DG *(the Director General of the Independent Television Authority)*. Did I not supply you with a list of telephone numbers, including mine, for you to contact if there was any doubt about the suitability of any part of a script?"

"You certainly did, Archie" I replied, trying to keep it all matey and light-hearted. Obviously, something had gone dreadfully wrong.

"And do you realise what you allowed to be transmitted last night?" barked Archie.

"Of course," I said. "There was the exciting exclusive on the Greville Wynn scoop, a light-hearted bit about the Archbishop of Canterbury and the same regarding the Queen, I think."

"Correct" said Archie in calm, but rather menacing tones.

My mind was gradually getting into a higher gear and it suddenly began to dawn on me that I – and Southern Television – were both in the proverbial.

"Now, let's take the first story regarding Greville Wynn being released by the Soviet Union, following secret and long negotiations with the British Government," continued Archie, icily. "Would you not consider that to be political?"

I had to agree that it was.

"And you recall that nothing of a political nature is allowable in a commercial?" I nodded and then, realising that I was on the telephone, muttered: "Yes".

"Now, let's talk about the Archbishop of Canterbury and his trouble with the verger."

"No need, Archie," I sighed. "No commercials may contain references to or highlight religious content. Right?"

"Exactly so," replied Archie. "And finally, may I bring up the reference to the Queen?"

"Please don't," I groaned, utterly mortified and increasingly concerned for my company's future and my own.

There was a long, long pause. I sweated.

Time passed very slowly until Archie eventually said: "Tony, I have my diary in front of me. Please open yours. And let us then agree on a date when I, as your guest, will enjoy a very long and very expensive lunch at the Savoy."

Later, I also took on the position of Head of Advertising Magazines at Southern. This department was created to exploit a loophole in the regulations relating to the amount of advertising permitted during each hour of broadcasting by creating a special twenty-minute programme in which mention of various products was worked into a simple storyline.

A good example of this ploy was 'Jim's Inn', starring Jimmy Hanley, who was married to Dinah Sheridan.

This story had a pub theme, with Jimmy as the landlord. A customer would enter, order a pint of Worthington, at which point there would be a discussion about the merits Worthington beer lasting sixty seconds. Then another customer would come in and, as he ordered his drink, would look at his watch.

"That's a nice watch," Jimmy would say.

"Yes," the customer would reply. "It's a Bulova." And he would then yack on about it for a further sixty seconds. The advertisers would be charged a special rate for this sort of exposure.

All the commercial television companies had their one 'admag' programme. A further two were produced by one of the major companies and networked to all the others. For the planning of this latter project, there was a Network Committee that met monthly at the head office of one of these companies.

I represented Southern Television and was required to attend a meeting at A.T.V (Association Television) near Marble Arch at 3.00pm one day. Having taken a very important client to lunch, I arrived there several minutes late.

I dashed straight up to the conference room, opened the door and sat down at the end of a large table. I opened my brief case and took out my papers. I knew everyone at these meetings and once I had settled myself down I looked up with the intention of apologising to the Chairman for my late arrival. At this point I found myself the focus of a dozen or so slightly perplexed faces, all except one of them utterly unfamiliar. The exception was Lord Lew Grade, the Chairman of A.T.V.

"Who are you?" he barked.

"Er, Salisbury, Southern Television," I stuttered.

"Well, be so good as to leave the room this instant," he ordered. "This is an A.T.V. board meeting and I hope you will be able to explain later what you are doing here."

I slunk out, muttering my apologies.

Back at Southern, meanwhile, the fun and games continued. Two of our very early newscasters were Dickie Davies, who went on to find fame as a sports presenter, and Julian Pettifer, who also went on to reach great heights, reporting on a wide variety of subjects from all around the world.

Julian, in particular, was a blessed with very good looks and was a great favourite with our lady viewers, from whom he received sackloads of fanmail. There was one elderly widow who wrote in on a regular basis, commenting favourably about his daily appearances on her screen. She would compliment him on his voice, his clothes, his lovely smile and his general manner.

Then, one day, he received a letter that ran along the following lines:

Dear Mr Pettifer,

Once again, I would like to say how very nice you looked on my television today. It is always such a pleasure to see you.

Kind regards etc etc

P.S. And how did you like my new curtains?

You have to understand that TV was still a relatively young medium in 1958 and the way in which it worked remained something of a mystery to the some of the more technologically-challenged members of the older generation. Even so, this story, which has since passed into television folklore, provided a startling illustration of the persuasive power of the box.

One of our biggest stars at Southern in the early days was Michael Miles, the host of the quiz show *Take Your Pick*, the great rival to Hughie Green's *Double Your Money*. *Take Your Pick* involved offering winning contestants the choice of either taking a guaranteed cash prize or opting to gamble by opening one of a selection of boxes that might contain tickets for a holiday in the Bahamas or something totally worthless such as a roll of toilet paper. The studio audience was primed to encourage the contestants to gamble by shouting: "Open the box!" The programmes would be recorded two-at-a-time down in Southampton and, once they had been edited, would be piped up to our London office for Michael Miles to view and approve.

His visits there would regularly bring him into contact with our Head of Administration, a colourful character who rejoiced in the name of Clarence D'eath – especially inappropriate in his case, given his background as a retired Chief Petty Officer who had spent most of his naval career in submarines.

A large man, with a loud rasping voice, Clarence would knock on my door and then march smartly into my office as if he were still in the service, standing to attention in front of my desk with papers and files under each arm while he reported on the day's routine activities, babbling on with the occasional 'Mr Salisbury, Sir!' thrown in as punctuation.

He also enjoyed regular lunchtime drinks every Friday with former naval colleagues at a club in Kensington. This often resulted in him returning to the office in a 'relaxed' state of mind. As most of us were usually in a similar condition this went largely unnoticed, until one day when I had not been out to lunch at all while he had obviously had an even more congenial session than usual with his ex-shipmates. As he stood rigidly to attention in front of me, papers and files began to slip from under his arms until my carpet was littered with bumpf while he carried on regardless, as if nothing was happening.

Clarence and Michael Miles had never got on and were forever complaining about each other's behaviour, although my sympathies were always with Clarence. On one occasion he burst into my office and, adopting his best NCO-to-Officer manner, announced: "Mr Salisbury! Sir! I have to report that I have just called Michael Miles a ****."

"I see, Clarence," I said, doing my best to keep a straight face. "Well, I think I'd better inform our Programme Controller of this, since Mr Miles is an important artiste."

I duly telephoned the Programme Controller and relayed Clarence's report.

There was a barely a moment's pause before the Controller replied: "Please tell Clarence that he has my full permission to call Michael Miles a **** as often as he likes."

Michael Miles died shortly after this incident and Clarence came into the office the next day with a worried look on his face.

"I have just had a call from Mrs Miles," he said. "She wants me to go to Michael's funeral as she understands I was one of his closest friends. She also said that she didn't want any unhappiness at the service and would like it to be fun. I don't quite understand what she means by saying she wants it to be fun. Has anybody got any ideas?"

"Well, perhaps you will all be given straws during the service and at the end whoever draws the shortest one will be invited to 'Open The Box'," someone rather mischievously suggested.

Among the more popular characters in the office in the early days of Southern was Graham Dowson, our first Advertising Sales Director. Graham had been a Squadron Leader during the War, a disc jockey in Texas and the sales director of the A. C. Nielson Company before joining Southern. He then left us to become marketing director at Rank, where he subsequently rose to become CEO, and it fell to me to organise his leaving party.

This entailed hiring the Oliver Messel Suite at The Dorchester, his favourite hotel, as well as ordering a gift from all of us from Gerrards, the jewellers. The party, complete with champagne and canapés, was due to begin at 6.oopm, with the presentation taking place at 8.oopm. Once again, it all sounded pretty straightforward. But no!

Graham entered my office that morning, rubbing his hands together gleefully. "Right, Tony, as it's my last day here why don't you and I and John Miell go out for a few drinks and a bite of lunch?" he suggested. I couldn't possibly refuse, but knowing what 'a few drinks and a bite of lunch' with Graham normally meant, my heart sank.

Graham decided to start the proceedings in my old stamping ground, The Antelope, off Eaton Square. We entered a virtually empty pub at 11.30am and Graham ordered what had recently become his favourite tipple. "Three pints of champagne with a double drambuie in each, please, Landlord."

After that it was my round, then John's. Then someone else we knew happened to pop in and foolishly asked us to have a drink on him. He was visibly shaken when we requested the same again and he realised what it was going to cost him!

The three of us had each now consumed four pints of champagne and eight drambuies.

"Just one more and then we'll go on to lunch," said Graham.

By this time John was slumped in a chair and becoming increasingly incoherent. I only kept reasonably steady because of my responsibilities that evening. Graham, meanwhile, was well into his stride and was singing his favourite aria from *Carmen*. He actually had a beautiful singing voice – good enough, I suspect, for him to have been a professional opera singer with the right training.

To my great relief, the landlord eventually called time and, picking up John, we made for the door. At this point, however, the landlord came over and said to Graham: "Excuse me, Sir, but aren't you from Scotland Yard?" Graham had this sort of effect on people. "That's quite right," he replied, showing remarkable presence of mind in the circumstances, his words only slightly slurred. "Allow me to introduce my two colleagues, Chief Inspector Salisbury and Detective Inspector Miell." John, only semi-conscious by this time, had to be held firmly in a standing position.

The landlord suddenly transformed himself into a cringing Uriah Heep and, while literally wringing his hands in the most obsequious manner, rather stupidly suggested: "I know it's somewhat irregular and illegal, Sir, but I wonder if you and your colleagues would care to join me for a drink?'

Yup! I'm afraid so. It was another pint of champagne and double drambuie!

My memories of what happened from then on are somewhat blurred, but others who were present that evening have helped to fill in some of the details.

Somehow we did all manage to make it to the Dorchester by 6.00pm, although I can't quite remember how I got there. The champagne and canapés were already being served as a suitably surprised Graham was delivered. The presentation was made and, as I have been reminded many times since, I made a garbled and largely incomprehensible speech.

Thankfully, there were no serious incidents, although it would seem that a number of goldfish were found floundering in Park Lane at around 9.00pm. A totally unsubstantiated theory suggested that they might have arrived there via the pool that was part of the Oliver Messel Suite, which just happened to overlook Park Lane. Total nonsense, I'm sure.

Graham, however, had still not had enough and, in characteristically generous fashion, suggested we all join him for dinner in the Terrace Restaurant. Wives and girlfriends were summoned and around thirty of us sat down to dinner. When the party did eventually start to break up the rest of us decided that we couldn't possibly accept Graham's hospitality on his last day in the job and insisted on picking up the tab between us.

This, coupled with the cost of the champagne reception, amounted to so much that it was quite impossible for the Dorchester to be paid in one go.

Years later I was told by the general manager that never in the hotel's history had a bill been settled over such a long period and with so many post-dated cheques. Altogether, it took roughly eight months and ninety separate instalments to clear the full amount, with several cheques bouncing along the way.

# VII

## ALL AT SEA

GRAHAM DOWSON is a great character in whose company I have spent many happy hours – but he can also be something of a liability if you go out on the town with him, as I discovered to my cost on more than one occasion. During the sixties, I took to winter cruising as the perfect way to get away from it all and enjoy a relaxing Christmas break, with all the facilities necessary to ensure maximum comfort, but without any Butlin-style pressure to join in various activities.

My first cruise holiday was aboard the Empress of England in 1960 and took me via Las Palmas and Dakar down across the Equator to Freetown and then back, stopping off at Madeira. Everything was fine until, on New Year's Eve, we got to Madeira. Here, we dropped anchor just outside the harbour at Funchal and a lighter then ferried passengers ashore.

Wandering along the quayside before taking a taxi into town, I came across another cruise ship, the Andes, which had already tied up there and, as I was passing, I happened to notice a familiar, well-built figure making his way down the gangplank. Much to my surprise, a second glance confirmed that it was indeed Graham.

By this time, he had been with Rank for a year or so. After an enthusiastic greeting, he insisted that I went back on board the Andes to have a glass or two of champagne before we ventured into the town. And so, at 10.30am, began a long and, to say the least, interesting day.

As we chatted in the bar, the captain of the liner came up and joined us. Making small talk, I asked him how the cruise was going.

"Don't ask me," he grinned. "Ask Graham. He took over my ship on the second day out!"

That figured, I thought.

We eventually disembarked and took a taxi to the world-famous Reids Hotel, associated over the years with the likes of Noel Coward, Somerset Maugham, Douglas Fairbanks Snr. and Winston Churchill. There, we had a few more glasses of champagne on the balcony overlooking the harbour before going on to enjoy an excellent lunch accompanied by a couple of bottles of wine and brandy.

Apart from its distinctive sherry-like wine and its beautiful flowers, Madeira is famed for the manufacture of cane furniture. In a mellow and relaxed mood by now, I suggested a shopping trip to a few of the local furniture shops, where I hoped to purchase some items for a house that I had recently moved into back in London. Graham agreed enthusiastically and, armed with my Amex card, we set off into the town centre.

Upon entering the first shop we were acquainted with the charming local custom whereby potential purchasers are invited to partake of a glass of Madeira. Altogether, we must have visited about eight different establishments in search of the two wastepaper baskets, the chair and the bedside table that I was after and at each one we were offered the same hospitality. I eventually found everything I was looking for, paying for each purchase with my credit card as we went along and getting an assurance that they would be shipped over together and delivered to the house in Ebury Street within six weeks.

Graham and I then retired to the Andes, where I used his cabin to have a wash and a short rest. Back in the bar, the captain explained that the New Year's Eve celebrations on Madeira were especially spectacular. Every single house would be lit up with fairy lights and the firework display, on the stroke of midnight, would be something to remember forever.

"Why not stay with us and watch the display from here?" suggested Graham.

I explained that, sadly, I couldn't really do that as my ship was due to sail at 12.15am and everybody was expected to be back on board by 11.45pm at the very latest.

At around 9.00pm Graham repeated the invitation and for good measure suggested I remain on the Andes for the rest of the voyage back to Southampton. He asked the captain if there was an empty cabin available and was told that there was and that I would be welcome to it.

"I can't," I persisted. "All my clothes, toiletries, books and other belongings are on my ship. And, anyway, it would cause chaos on board."

My resolve was ebbing away with the contents of each fresh glass of champagne and I was persuaded to stay at least for dinner. Needless to say, I then lost track of time until everybody started streaming up on deck to watch the fireworks, at which point I looked at my watch to discover to my horror that it was almost midnight. The final 11.45pm deadline for my return to my own ship had passed and, despite the offer of a cabin aboard the Andes, I realised that it was clearly ridiculous simply to jump ship without informing anyone – not to mention the small matter of what would happen to all my belongings.

As I stumbled off in search of the Andes' jovial captain to explain my predicament, the firework display began. The entire island suddenly erupted in a series of enormous, deafening explosions, screeching rockets and crackling, multi-coloured starbursts. Every individual house seemed have its own display as well as the main one in the centre of town. And above all this noise a ship's hooter could be heard blasting away. It was the Empress of England. She was a passenger short and she was due to sail in fifteen minutes.

"I've got a bit of a problem here," I bellowed in the ear of the captain, when I eventually located him up on the bridge.

"Don't panic," he replied cheerily. "I'll radio your ship and tell them that you are with me and that I am about to send you out to them in my barge."

Thanking everyone profusely, I stepped into the captain's barge a few minutes later and was delivered to the Empress of England, whose sailing time had been delayed all because of little me!

The barge came alongside the ship, a gangplank was lowered and I scrambled aboard to be greeted by three sour looking and extremely angry senior ship's officers, who, without a word of welcome, pointed me towards my cabin.

There is an epilogue to this particular story. Some weeks later, I was entertaining a friend to lunch at the house in Ebury Street when the doorbell rang. I answered it to find a uniformed man at the door, saying that he had an overseas delivery for me. I looked past him to where a vast pantechnicon was parked in the road outside. He and two mates then proceeded to spend the next half-an-hour unloading a dozen cane wastepaper baskets, a couple of settees, ten chairs, six coffee tables, four bedside tables ... and two bird cages!

I was left to reflect that eight glasses of complimentary Madeira on top of champagne, wine and brandy obviously tend to cloud one's judgement at bit.

Undeterred by my experiences in Funchal, I went on similar cruises for several Christmases running and generally found them very pleasant and relaxing, although they never seemed to be entirely free of incident and one encountered some very strange and unlikely characters.

In this respect, my voyage on the S.S. France got off to an interesting start. Having found and settled into my cabin, I set off to explore the ship. It was huge, with at least ten deck levels, and it seemed that every time I pushed a lift button to any of these decks the doors would open to reveal a bar. This was good news, so I continued to press buttons.

At the last stop I decided to get out and have a whisky. I sat on a stool at the bar and quickly got into conversation with a very interesting and extrovert character with only one ear, who turned out to be a Monte Carlo rally driver. After we had been chatting for about an hour we noticed a person sitting nearby who seemed to be in a state of deep depression, his head sunk in his hands. I made an effort to engage him in conversation, whereupon he stared at me through bleary eyes for a full minute without uttering a word.

"Please don't speak to me, Sir," he sighed eventually. "I'm unhappy. I've lost my girlfriend, I am going to get very drunk and I am from Peru." He included the last part of this remark as if it were somehow associated with the other parts, although the relevance wasn't at all clear. We turned away and left him to it.

My new acquaintance and I went down to dinner together and agreed to meet again in the same bar at 11.00am the next day. I arrived at the appointed time to find our Peruvian friend seated on the same bar stool, but in state of even greater distress, his clothes soaking wet and showing evidence of having been quite badly burned.

"I know I shall regret asking this," I said. "But you seem to be a little the worse for wear?"

After a moment's pause, he sighed deeply. "I suppose I should consider myself lucky," he said. "I had a few more drinks after you left and then, at midnight, tried to find my way back to my cabin. But wherever I went I kept coming back to this bar. It was all very confusing. So I thought – to hell with it! I'll sleep on one of those sun loungers out on deck. I went out there, found one and lay down on it. Then I lit a cigarette and that's the last I can remember until I woke up at about 6.00am."

He emptied his glass and ordered another drink.

"I must have dropped off to sleep with the cigarette still alight and it then dropped onto my jacket and I caught fire," he continued. "That's when I got really lucky, because it started raining and the downpour put me out."

He turned away again and spent the rest of the cruise on the same stool in the same bar, gazing unhappily into space and rebuffing all attempts at conversation. We never did find out any more about him.

You can never be quite sure who will be on your table for dinner during these cruises, which, as far as I am concerned, is part of the appeal. On the Canberra, I found myself on a table of ten, hosted by the First Officer. Among my fellow diners were an obviously wealthy, 89-year-old woman and a very much younger man, who turned out to be on their honeymoon! Accompanying this rather unlikely couple were the old lady's lawyer, a chap named George, and his young blonde wife, also on their honeymoon.

The old lady, very striking to look at despite her age, couldn't wait to introduce her husband, a tall, well-built Greek in his late thirties. Unlike everyone else, he was not wearing a dinner jacket, but was dressed instead in an open-necked shirt, unbuttoned to expose a hairy chest on which nestled a large gold crucifix. Both his wrists were encircled with gold bracelets and he also sported a chunky gold watch. Four of his fingers were adorned with enormous gold rings.

The look on my face must have resembled that of P. G. Woodhouse's Bertie Wooster when urged by his Aunt Agatha to: "Stop gaping, Bertie, and shut your mouth."

The formidable old lady dominated our table from the start. Even the First Officer, who seemed quite a gregarious character, was rendered pretty well speechless. At the same time, I couldn't help noticing that her jewellery-bedecked gigolo of a husband seemed to be openly hero-worshipped by the ship's Greek stewards, who, when not actually serving you, tended to walk around holding hands! At every opportunity, they would beam at him, pat him on the back and give him the thumbs up. I assumed they were merely showing some sort of patriotic solidarity with their fellow countryman until it was revealed that he had been the wine waiter on the previous cruise, during which he had 'served' the lady who was now his wife.

The situation then took another bizarre twist on the fourth night. I was sitting next to the lawyer's wife when she suddenly confided: "I'm terribly worried about George – I'm beginning to think he might be queer!"

We didn't see much of her after this, but George and the old lady's Greek husband seemed to be getting along famously together!

To add to all this, it then became obvious that the First Officer himself was also gay. I seemed to be trapped in mid-Atlantic in a ship where the ship's crew, half the passengers and some of the officers were raging homosexuals.

The final straw came when I attended a cocktail party at which I got chatting to the Chief Engineer, a large, bearded Scotsman who bore a passing resemblance to the actor James Robertson Justice. We were sitting next to each other with a glass of champagne when a hairy hand clamped itself on my knee. "Fancy a night cap later on, laddie?" he muttered.

At this point I decided I'd had enough and when we reached Madeira, once again our last port of call on the way home, I decided to fly back to England. I took a taxi to the tiny airport to find out when the next flight was scheduled. It turned out that the only one that day was due to leave in half an hour and that seats were available. Without further ado, I bought a ticket and got straight on the plane.

It was only when I was in the air that I realised the implications of once again jumping ship without prior warning. Luckily, with the help of a friendly stewardess, I was able to persuade the pilot to contact the airport and ask somebody there to get in touch with the ship to inform the captain about my sudden change of plan. Also, to pass on the name of a friend on board who would settle any outstanding bills, pack my clothes and have them delivered to my home. This rescue mission was later to cost me a couple of extremely long and expensive lunches.

Not the happiest of holidays, then. But, as I had already discovered by this time, far worse things can happen at sea. The truth of this was brought home to me by two incidents, both involving my mother.

She had gone into something of a decline in the years after the war. For a start, her financial situation had been somewhat undermined when her rich and indulgent father, three months before he died in 1945, contrived to marry the nurse who had been attending to him in his final years. The provisions that he then made for her in his will had the effect of severely diluting my mother's own inheritance, much to her irritation. Not that she was destitute, by any means.

She and SF2, Mark Roddick, had been living down in Gloucestershire in Coln St Aldwyn manor, part of the estate of Earl St Aldwyn, a great friend who had served with SF2 in the Queen's Bays (2nd Dragoon Guards). They now moved to County Kerry, where the Trust helped to purchase a beautiful house on Curragh Lake, near Killarney, called Ard Na Sidhe – the Hill of the Fairies.

Here they had a couple of steeplechasers, trained by Vincent O'Brien. SF2 had been a renowned amateur rider in his day, winning the Grand Military Gold Cup three times on three different horses, all of which he trained himself. He was also a highly acclaimed salmon fisherman, so Eire suited him very well.

My mother, however, did not feel nearly so much at home in this beautiful but rather remote location so far away from her old social stamping grounds and she became increasingly depressed. At the same time, SF2 began to show signs of mental instability as the shrapnel that had been left in his head as a result of his war wound started to move around.

With his condition deteriorating, they eventually sold Ard Na Sidhe – since converted into a country house hotel – and moved to a permanent suite in the Hermitage Hotel in Monte Carlo. Here, Mark got progressively worse and soon had to be hospitalised. He remained in hospital for the next five years, unable to recognise his wife when she went to visit him. His death, in 1960, was probably a merciful release.

Following his cremation, my mother then decided, for some reason, to have his ashes scattered at sea. As ever, this was not quite as straightforward as one might have supposed. For a start, the French regulations apparently required the ceremony to be conducted outside the three-mile limit. Mummy duly arranged to borrow a yacht belonging to Russian exile Prince Beria and then invited the director of the Monte Carlo casino and a few other select friends to join her on board for the ceremony, which was to be conducted by an English clergyman. What followed could well be described as the blackest of French comedy.

I was not present for the occasion, but heard the full story from my mother herself. At the end of the short service, for which she had quite understandably fortified herself with numerous gin-and-tonics, the time came for her to scatter the ashes. She managed that bit alright, but then went on to heave a large wreath overboard – and, unfortunately, followed it into the water.

Some say that the yacht hit a wave and lurched at the wrong moment, others that the gin and tonics contributed, while the more charitable maintained that she had made a conscious decision to join her husband in his watery grave. Whatever the cause of the mishap, she was eventually hauled to safety and everyone retired to the wardroom for sustenance as the boat returned to the harbour.

Her own health started to deteriorate very quickly after that. She soon became bedridden and it was only prescribed drugs, along with the odd drink or two, that kept her going. She eventually died in

1964, and left instructions that her ashes, too, should be scattered at sea.

I flew over to make the necessary arrangements. Following her cremation in Marseilles, I organised the loan of a yacht in Cannes, and invited pretty much the same group of friends and the same English vicar who had been present at SF2's funeral to attend the scattering of her ashes later in the week. These, in the meantime, were sent by post from Marseille to Cannes, where I had to collect them at the Post Office. The urn was inside a box, wrapped in brown paper and tied with string. On the way to the yacht I decided I needed a drink to steady my nerve. I sat in a bar on the seafront, Mummy on the counter, and downed a couple of very welcome cognacs before going on to join everybody else aboard the yacht.

Unfortunately, it then turned out that the sea was too rough. We were unable to make it out to the three-mile limit and had to return to the harbour, sitting around the wardroom table, drinking champagne, with Mummy's urn in the middle, while we discussed where she should spend the night until we could try again the next morning. The general view was that the best place would be the yacht's large refrigerator, where she would feel at home amongst the bottles of champagne. However, the English vicar thought it would be preferable if he took her to his church for safekeeping.

The next day we set off again in calmer conditions and this time succeeded in reaching the three-mile limit. At the end of the short ceremony I then took the urn, which was actually just a square tin box, and lowered it over the end of the boat. Unfortunately, I had rather stupidly failed to appreciate that a sealed tin box would not sink. Mummy started drifting about. Grabbing a screwdriver, I ended up stabbing away at her floating coffin until she quietly disappeared.

Somehow, it seemed a bizarrely appropriate ending to a short but eventful life, lived at a fast, furious and often recklessly hedonistic pace.

She was just fifty-nine.

# VIII

## STARS, BARS AND STICKY WICKETS

T THE HEIGHT of the so-called swinging sixties, London was probably the most exciting city in the world and as a reasonably well-off bachelor in his thirties, with a good job in television and a flat just off the King's Road in Chelsea, I was perfectly placed to make the most of it.

I had found the flat through a colleague at Southern Television, Biddy Martin. Biddy was in charge of the Admags department that I myself was to take over at a later stage. She was aware that I was looking for a place of my own, after years of sharing with various other people, and when a flat fell vacant in the block where she was living she tipped me off.

On the day that I moved in I got back from the office, changed into my pyjamas, poured myself a large whisky and settled down for a quiet, relaxing evening in front of the television. Then the telephone rang. It was Biddy, welcoming me to my new home and suggesting that I pop downstairs to her place for a drink. I explained that I was in my pyjamas and that she would have to wait while I changed. "Oh, don't bother," she said. "Just grab a dressing gown and come as you are. Nobody will notice."

With a bottle of Scotch clutched in my hand, I slipped down the stairs and across the small courtyard to Biddy's flat. On the way, I passed a chap in a bowler hat, standing, half hidden, behind a pillar.

Biddy and I had quite a few drinks. She then cooked an omelette and at around 10.00pm I left with the now nearly empty bottle of

Scotch. As I crossed the courtyard I noticed that the man with the bowler hat was still there. I walked up the stairs, into my flat and settled into my armchair once again to watch the box. It was only then that I began to wonder about the bowler-hatted gent downstairs – and suddenly it all started clicking into place. I knew that Biddy was separated from her husband. The mystery man was obviously a private detective, hired to come up with evidence of her being up to 'naughties'. And I had conveniently obliged him by arriving at her flat in pyjamas and a dressing gown and carrying a bottle of whisky and had proceeded to spend the next three hours there. I recounted my suspicious to Biddy next day. Her reaction was very lucid and calm: "Oh God, Oh God, Oh God!"

However, nothing happened and I decided that I had panicked unnecessarily. Without mentioning Biddy by name, I related this story some time later to a few colleagues in my local pub, The Antelope. Among the group was one chap I didn't know, a friend of one of the others present. When I'd finished he said: "Are you by any chance talking about Biddy Martin?"

"Er, yes, as a matter of fact I am," I admitted, suddenly feeling very apprehensive.

He burst out laughing. "Well, I'm the husband and I'm very pleased to meet you!" he chuckled. "As it happens, you were quite right – it was a private detective hired by me to check up on Biddy. But in the end I didn't need to make use of his evidence because Biddy and I sorted everything out very amicably."

I made a mental note to be a little bit more careful in future and to make sure that I observed conventional dress codes at all times, even if everybody else seemed to be casting off all their inhibitions amid the heady atmosphere of the new permissive society.

My social life was as hectic as ever, while my sporting interests, previously confined almost exclusively to cricket, were briefly expanded to include active involvement in horse racing, as an owner!

This came about purely by chance. The story actually starts in the conference room at Southern Television's London office, where I and three of my senior colleagues from the Advertising Sales department were meeting to discuss a new rate card for the coming autumn season.

Members of a star-studded Capital Radio XI, including (left to right) Jo Rice, Kevin Ward, Tim Rice (who had his own programme on Capital at the time), actor Gerald Harper, DJ Tommy Vance and me, all clearly demonstrating the convivial spirit in which we approached our cricket and (BELOW) a couple of spectators getting carried away with the sheer thrill of a match between Capital and a team from Speldhurst, Kent, the home village of Liza Myers, my PA at Capital at the time.

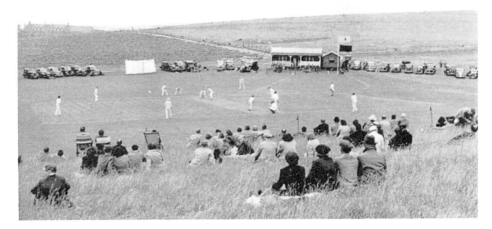

30-10-84.

Mr. Tony Salisbury,
Falmer Road,
NOTTINGDEAN.

Dear Tony,

   I received your correspondence dated 19th October asking me to become one of the "friends" of Rottingdean Cricket Club.

   As I am 77 and live 12000 miles away it would be transparent to everybody that this would be nothing more than a publicity gimmick and as such I think it would be more honest and sensible if I respectfully decline and leave tangible support for the Club to English residents who could conceivably have some association with the Club.

     Yours faithfully,

*Don Bradman*

TOP: *Rottingdean's historic downland cricket ground, where I made my first appearance in 1948.*

ABOVE: *(sixth from left) Walking out in 1950 with a team captained by Ernest Beard (with stick) and including 'Pop' Coates (second left) and Henry Blyth (far right), from whom I took over as Captain in 1964.*

LEFT: *The letter received from Sir Donald Bradman after I had written to him asking if he would consider lending his support to our historic club by becoming one of the official Friends Of Rottingdean.*

*Tossing up with opposing captains Joe Smith (left) and Derek Roberts (right) before the start of the 18th-century match staged at Rottingdean in 1986 and (BELOW, in white tuxedo) outside The Plough, the Rottingdean village pub, with LWT sales colleagues who attended my Lord's Taverners dinner there. With his head on my shoulder is Patrick Shervington, the Director of the Lord's Taverners at the time.*

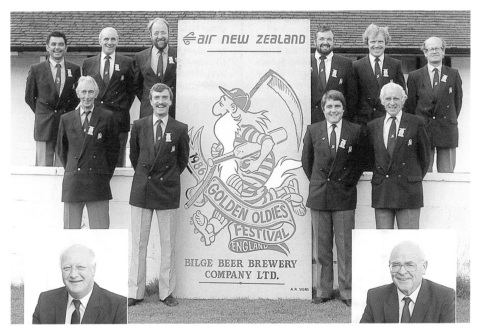

ABOVE: *With Sir Gary Sobers at a Lord's Taverners charity bus presentation.* RIGHT: *Gary goes down on one knee to demonstrate the art of 'Lilliput Cricket' as played on the streets of the West Indies.*

FACING PAGE, TOP: *Me (in red trousers) with members of the International Golden Oldies organising committee,* (MIDDLE, LEFT) *Leslie Crowther with the Mayor of Hove and West Indies star Charlie Griffith and* (MIDDLE, RIGHT) *me receiving a cheque from Dave Holford.* OPPOSITE: *Me with the legendary Ray Lindwall (centre) and a fellow Aussie.*

*At another favourite restaurant, Caraffini, with former Southern TV Sales and Marketing Director and eventual business partner Graham Dowson and (BELOW) with some of the players who took part in a benefit match between a Lord's Taverners XI and former Sussex captain John Barclay's XI. I'm on the extreme left, next to Leslie Crowther, with, among others, former England players John Edrich (eighth from left) and John Snow (second from right). With the bat is John Barclay and on his left is actor Michael Jayston, who took over from me as President of the East Sussex region of the Lord's Taverners.*

*Celebrating 30 years of Capital Radio on Dickie Attenborough's sweeping staircase and (BELOW) with fellow heads of media sales (left to riht) Tony Vickers, Sales Director at various times of TV-AM, Capital Radio and SKY BRMB, John Miell, Sales Director of Southern TV and John Fox, Sales Director of Meridien TV and then Managaing Director of BMRB. In the middle is Mrs Fox. I was with LWT at the time.*

ABOVE: *During my brief spell as a racehorse owner with Gallant Squire, bought with the winnings from a lucky night at the casino, and* (BELOW) *in relaxed mood at Scalini, a favourite restaurant in Chelsea.*

We worked at it until 1.00pm and sent out for sandwiches. At the same time, we opened a bottle of gin. We drank the gin and ate the sandwiches. Then, as is normal in good society – or certainly was in those days – we opened a bottle of brandy after our snack and continued our deliberations. Somehow, the bottle was emptied and another opened. We continued our work.

At 8.00pm, having polished off the second bottle, we sensibly decided to call it a day. I left the office near Victoria and, for no particular reason, wandered off in the direction of Piccadilly and eventually happened to find myself outside the Palm Beach Casino in Berkeley Square, an establishment of which my brother-in-law had made me a member just a month before.

I had £10 on me. I stumbled into a large room full of various gaming tables and, mainly because I desperately needed to sit down somewhere, perched on a stool at the American roulette table. I fell off. Two waiters helped me back into my seat and I plonked my entire £10 on red. Red came up. I left my winnings there. Red came up again. I left it there. Red came up again. I fell off my stool again. The waiters replaced me. Red just kept on coming up.

My memory about subsequent events is hazy, but it seems that a cricketer pal of mine, Larry O'Callaghan happened to be playing roulette at another table and, hearing the commotion, came over to find out what all the fuss was about. He and the friend he was with arrived in time to witness me being put back on my stool for the third time.

Seeing that I had piles of chips on red and realising I was not 100% in command of my faculties, they made an attempt to be helpful.

"For God's sake be sensible, Tony, and get out of here right now," said Larry.

"**** off," I said, sliding downwards again.

The two of them now decided on immediate action. Taking me by my arms, they lifted me bodily off my stool and frogmarched me along to the cashier's office. Here, I produced chips from every available pocket. The cashier counted them, wrote a cheque and handed it to me.

I'm told that I inspected it very closely and then, swaying ever so slightly, handed it back with the slurred comment: "That's awfully kind of you, old man, but you seem to have made a mistake. You have added an extra 'o' on this cheque."

"I can assure you we have not, Sir," he said with a smile, once again presenting me with the cheque for £3,000. And this was 1964!

In the sober light of the next morning, I started reflecting on what to do with my windfall. After very little deliberation I decided to blow the lot on a mink jacket for my girlfriend, Jill … and a race-horse for myself!

I had often thought that it would be great fun to own a chaser. I had been brought up with polo ponies and, as I have already mentioned, SF2 – Mark Roddick – had been a great amateur rider in his day and had later owned three horses, all trained by Vincent O'Brien.

A friend introduced me to Alan Oughton, who trained at Finedon, where Ryan Price had his stables. Alan had been a champion chase jockey in his time and was a most delightful and amusing character. Of the many stories that were told about him, the one I liked best concerned a New Year's Day event at Plumpton.

Alan, it seems, was riding the 3/1 favourite, but he had been celebrating New Year's Eve until the very, very early hours and, had he been breathalysed at the start of the race, he would undoubtedly have been found to be way over the limit. The three-mile chase involved two-and-half laps of the Plumpton circuit, which meant that it only finished when you passed the winning post for the third time. Alan was leading by about ten lengths when he passed it for the second time, whereupon he dropped the reins, waving to acknowledge what he thought were the cheers of the crowd and then heading towards the winner's enclosure before realising his mistake as the rest of the field swept by for the final lap. For some time after that, racing at Plumpton on New Year's Day was dropped.

I explained to Alan that I had about £800 to spend on a horse and reckoned I could just about afford £30 a week for trainer's fees. And for that I was hoping that I could get a chaser who just might become a Grand National prospect.

Alan was not entirely happy with this arrangement. He knew that when a trainer buys for his owner, he always gets the blame if it doesn't win. I swore to him that this would never be the case as far as I was concerned and he duly went off and found a three year old by Happy Knight out of Bridesmaid. The pedigree was encouraging and the price as per budget.

At 17.2 hands, he was just about the biggest racehorse of the time. The first thing we had to decide was what to call him. Given his parents' names, my first suggestion was Wet Dream. Not surprisingly, nobody thought that was a very good idea. I then toyed with Dropping Back, thinking mischievously of all the confusion that would cause for Peter O'Sullevan and the other race commentators. I was sent back to the drawing board. Realising that the horse should have some dignity, the publicity manager at Southern Television came up with Gallant Squire. Perfect.

Gallant Squire had a couple of problems, not counting the two between his legs, which affected his jumping. The plain fact was that he was extremely eccentric. For instance, no one could get on board without first caressing his tongue. If you didn't do that, you were up in the air and on your back in the mud in a flash. The second was that he jumped all hurdles as though they were Becher's Brook, resulting in the rest of the field soon leaving him a distance behind.

On one occasion he was entered for a hurdle race at Windsor in which the Queen Mother also had a horse running. Jill and I mingled near her in the paddock as we saw our jockey, Buck Jones, into the saddle. The Queen Mum then went off with Alan Oughton to watch the race in the stands.

"Mr. Oughton," she said at one point, smiling that sweet smile of hers. "I understand you have a horse in this race which had some trouble being named. Do tell me the full story."

"I would prefer not to, Ma'am," replied Alan

"No, I really would like to know," she persisted.

"I really would prefer not to, if you don't mind, Ma'am," repeated Alan. "It's rather embarrassing."

"I command you," insisted the Queen Mother.

Alan told the story as delicately as he could and I understand that the she thought it was quite a giggle.

I'm afraid my career as an owner never really took off. Gallant Squire never quite lived up to expectations. Vet fees were very heavy, training fees had to go up and then there was an outbreak of foot and mouth that resulted in all racing being cancelled for a time. It was all too much. My budget was soon exhausted and Gallant Squire was sold to a syndicate, never to be heard of again. However, it was an interesting experience and good fun while it lasted.

At the same time, the gambling spree sparked by that initial success on the roulette wheel was also mercifully short-lived. My beginner's luck definitely gave me the taste for more. I went back to the casino the following week and turned £50 into £800. The next week £100 became £700. Then I started to lose. I'm pleased to say that it didn't take long for me to realise just what a mug's game it is and I quit long before my losses became serious. I was helped in this by the fact that I very soon found the whole atmosphere of casinos to be joyless and totally soul-destroying. Those I frequented for that brief spell seemed to be populated mostly by elderly widows, who would sit there for hours on end, watching each turn of the wheel with a deadpan look of bored resignation. No smiles, no chat. All utterly depressing.

In 1960 I flew to New York to give my younger sister Amanda away at her wedding. Graham Dowson, my boss at Southern Television at the time, had very conveniently contrived to send me over there to compile a report on American commercial television so that I could legitimately claim that it was a business trip. As a result, I was able to stay on in Amanda and Tom's Manhattan apartment for a further week after the wedding, while they were on honeymoon.

Helping me with my report were two senior executives from A.C. Nielsen, the largest television research company in the States. One evening, after an enjoyable dinner, they took me to a bar where, after a while, I assured them that I would be quite happy on my own if they wanted to get back home.

That would have been fine in London, but, of course, I was in a New York bar with no idea where I was exactly. On leaving, I stepped out into a March blizzard. I started to walk, hoping to find a taxi. Nothing. I turned a corner and noticed I was in a street called Basin Street East. That rang an immediate bell as being the home of jazz. With my head down, I continued up the street through the driving snow until I found myself outside a well-lit doorway, through which could be glimpsed a welcoming bar. I entered, cold and wet and relieved to be able to seek refuge from the weather, only to find that the place was virtually empty apart from two barmen. The time was already 10.30pm but, being a live jazz club that catered for a late-night clientele, it had only just opened, they explained.

I ordered a large whisky and they immediately became very chatty, intrigued by my English accent. They suggested that I should hang around for a while until the weather improved, taking the opportunity at the same time to listen to what they promised would be some very good music. I was then shown to a table on the edge of a small balcony, beneath which was a small dance floor and a rostrum for the band, who had yet to arrive.

The bar started to fill up and I was joined at my table by an inebriated New York businessman, who, without a word, pulled a wad of dollar bills from his pocket and threw them down on the table. The barman, obviously familiar with this procedure, came over with a large bourbon, set it down and took the necessary money. Not a word was exchanged. After this routine had been repeated, I thought it would be polite to try and make conversation, particularly as it was usually the gregarious Americans who took the initiative.

I introduced myself, remarked on what an interesting place it seemed to be and inquired if he was a regular at the club. He fixed me with a drunken stare and made it abundantly clear that he was not in the mood for conversation of any kind, growling at me in that blunt, nasal and rather aggressive tone of voice that first-time visitors to New York often find so disconcerting.

Taking this less than subtle hint, I settled back instead to watch people arriving below me. Eventually the members of the band sauntered onto the rostrum one by one and, as I glanced at the first of them, I could hardly believe my eyes. It was Gene Krupa, probably the greatest drummer of all time. Behind him, to my even greater amazement, came Louis Armstrong. To cap it all, the vocalist turned out to be none other than Peggy Lee!

There I sat, within touching distance of three of the greatest stars of the jazz age, listening to them in the perfectly atmospheric surroundings of a smoke-filled bar in Basin Street, with a mournful, drunken American slumped beside me.

Through my work in television, I often came into contact with quite major stars, but I have never felt entirely at ease in their company. In this respect I got off to a bad start when I went out for a time with the daughter of the actor Jack Hulbert. I was walking along the Brompton Road with her one day after a session in the Bunch of Grapes when she suddenly pointed across the street and cried: "Oh, look! There's daddy." She dragged me over and introduced us and I was so completely at a loss for words that I simply blurted out the first thing that came into my head, which was: "Do you know, Sir, everybody says I look a bit like you. I don't really, do I?" An awkward silence followed and I still blush to recall the withering look of total contempt that he gave me.

I've also learned over the years to be wary of approaching celebrities to express admiration for their performances. I had a date with a girlfriend in the Rib Room at the Carlton Tower Hotel at 6.30pm one evening and, having got there about half-an-hour early, I decided to have a quick pint in the pub just around the corner. The place was empty except for one man who was sitting at the bar, hunched over his drink. It was Lee Marvin.

I had just been to see the film Cat Ballou, for which he received an Oscar. Since there was nobody else around, I turned to him after ordering my pint and said with a smile: "Please excuse me, Mr. Marvin, but I have just seen Cat Ballou and I thought it was absolutely marvellous. I'd like to congratulate you on your Oscar."

A bleary-eyed face looked up at me.

"Why don't you f*** off?" he growled.

As you might expect, I got a much more subtle rebuff from Sir Lawrence Olivier (as he then was) when I ventured to compliment him on one of his great performances. After another weekend of cricket at Rottingdean, I was returning to London one Monday morning on the Brighton Belle, as usual, when I looked up from my paper to see the great man sitting opposite me in the First Class buffet. He regularly used the train to commute to London from his home in Brighton, but this was the first time I had actually seen him on it.

He had just come back from Moscow, where his performance as Othello had been rapturously acclaimed. It was all over the papers and I decided that congratulations would be in order. Then I had second thoughts and held my tongue. Finally, approaching East Croydon, I plunged in.

"Sir Lawrence," I said. "I must congratulate you on your success in Russia."

There was no response. He continued to stare past me, with a faraway look in his eye. Then he slowly lowered his head, sank it into his hands and let out a deep sigh.

In a flash, I realised what I had done. It was obvious. In his head he was rehearsing his lines for whatever work he was travelling to London to undertake that day. I shrank back into my seat, sweating with embarrassment.

It wasn't until several minutes later, as we were approaching Victoria at the end of the journey, that he lifted his head from his hands and, with the faintest of smiles, mouthed the words: "Thank you."

At the opposite extreme, the most accommodating star I ever encountered was Erroll Flynn. I met him only once – in the loo of the Astor nightclub in Berkeley Square! It was about 2.00am and I had enjoyed a very congenial evening, which probably explains why, on this occasion, I rather uncharacteristically threw all caution and decorum to the winds.

Finding myself standing in the next stall I couldn't resist taking the advantage of the opportunity to check out one of Hollywood's most persistent and salacious rumours. "Good morning, Mr Flynn," I said politely. "I hope you won't think it too personal, but may I ...?"

I didn't need to go any further. Erroll grinned broadly. "Be my guest," he drawled.

I peeked over the partition – and was somewhat reassured by what I saw.

While we're on that particular subject, it was at around this time that I noticed that Sotheby's were having a sale of Napoleonic memorabilia and as I was fascinated by Napoleon, having recently been to Mal Maison, the house just outside Paris where he lived with Josephine, I sent off for the catalogue. This listed Lot 87 as: 'An item of Napoleon, nestled in a snuff box'.

Apparently, after he died, various parts of his body were cut off and kept as souvenirs. Lot 87 was a very private part. I decided that I had to have it. Not for any unpleasant reasons or even as something to treasure, but because it would be a wonderful 'tool', if you'll excuse the expression, to use at parties whenever the conversation happened to dry up. To bring out the snuff box with the casual comment: "Anyone like to see Napoleon's prick?" would be sure to have a dramatic effect.

I decided I could go up as high as £400. It was eventually knocked down at £30,000!

Meanwhile, I was continuing to enjoy all sorts of fun and games on the cricket pitch, especially when it came to the occasional 'benefit' games organised on behalf of long-serving Sussex county players.

Before the introduction of one-day cricket and those horrible pyjamas in which the players are kitted out, county beneficiaries used to arrange a number of Sunday fixtures against selected village teams capable of attracting a sufficient number of supporters to make the occasion financially viable. Rottingdean was a popular venue for such matches, since we usually managed to attract about 1,000 spectators and could also be relied upon to give the beneficiary's XI an enjoyable game, with loads of hospitality.

Sussex in the fifties and sixties were a successful and glamorous side and had won the original Gillette Cup. They had many famous players, including a number of extrovert personalities – Ted Dexter, Jim Parks, Rupert Webb, Les Lenham, Ken Suttle, Alan Oakman and Don Smith, to mention but a few.

England wicket keeper and batsman Jim Parks' benefit was particularly memorable. I was captain of Rottingdean on that occasion and we arranged to entertain the Sussex XI to lunch beforehand at the Plough Inn. The Plough was next to the pond, the green, the church and the house in which Rudyard Kipling, the village's most famous son, had once lived. Beer and wine flowed freely and a jolly good time was had by all and sundry, after which we reported to the ground for a 2.30pm start. It was a beautiful August Bank Holiday Sunday, with the large crowd seated on deck chairs supplied by the County ground.

Jim Parks and I went out to the square to toss up. For obvious reasons, it is traditional for the beneficiary's side to bat first. This is to guard against the danger of the game being over too quickly in the event of the village side being bowled out for a paltry total and to ensure that people get a chance to see all the star batsmen in action. I won the toss and duly elected to put the opposition in to bat.

However, things then started to go seriously awry when it became clear that our opening bowler, Jack Goss, was causing the Sussex batsmen considerable trouble. Jack was a first class bowler on his day and had once taken 178 wickets in a single season, probably a village cricket club record. On this particular occasion he was in devastating form and before long he had reduced Jim's all-star XI to 60 for 5. This was bad news all round. The crowd, who had come to see an exhibition of flashing stroke play from the professionals, were disappointed and the atmosphere was getting decidedly frosty as, one by one, the big names were sent back to the pavilion with egg on their faces. I decided to make a diplomatic bowling change and took Jack off.

It is never very sensible to take off a bowler who is bowling well against top class batsmen. It was particularly unwise to do this to Jack Goss. The language was such that some mothers a hundred yards away could be seen clasping their hands over their children's ears.

When I then compounded the felony by putting myself on in his place, Jack was even more outraged. Mothers now started shepherding their children out of the ground altogether. However, my decision had the desired effect insofar as it enabled the remaining Sussex batsmen, particularly Jim Parks, to hit the ball out of the ground with regularity, much to the delight of the spectators, who showed their appreciation by throwing ever more generous handfuls of coins into the collection sheet that was being carried round.

Jim's eventual dismissal provided one of the more amusing highlights of the innings. Playing only his second game for Rottingdean was a young chap called Chris, who had joined us straight from Eton. I won't give his full name for reasons that will shortly become clear. Chris's father had worked as the starter at steeplechase race meetings. He loved this job and was aghast when told that he would be required to retire at sixty, regardless of the fact that he was still mentally alert and physically fit.

He developed a plan. Twenty minutes before the last race of his final meeting he had a word in the ear of a jockey who was riding a 20-1 outsider. As all the horses lined up behind the tape, this jockey hung back about twenty lengths before eventually starting to trot towards the line. The trot became a canter, the canter became a gallop and by the time he came up to the line he was in full flight. At that very moment, Chris's dad sprung the tape and they were off. Thanks to this flying start, the runaway outsider had already stormed into a healthy lead by the end of first furlong and went on to win by a distance. Having backed the horse heavily, Chris's dad retired a happy man.

Back at Rottingdean, Chris was fielding on the mid wicket boundary, just in front of a group of spectators made up mostly of women and children, when Jim Parks took an almighty swipe at a juicy long hop. The ball soared to an enormous height and as it then began to descend it was obvious that it was going to fall neatly into Chris's waiting hands.

Realising this as it came his way, Chris looked up and shouted: "F****** hell!" Then, remembering that there were women and children within earshot and being a polite and well brought up young man, he turned to the spectators behind him and called out "I'm terribly sorry, ladies" before calmly turning back to take the catch.

By the time the tea interval arrived, our illustrious visitors were able to declare with a respectable total of over 200 runs on the board. As our opening batsmen then prepared to walk out to the wicket and I went back into the pavilion to pad up, ready to go in at No 3 as usual, I heard someone say: "Look at John Snow – is he trying to be funny?" John Snow was England's leading fast bowler at the time, renowned as a fearsomely aggressive and intimidating competitor. I glanced out of the window to see him standing by our sightscreen, tossing the ball from hand to hand. "Oh, no," I said straightaway. "He is not being funny. He's going to bowl flat out. We obviously upset him by doing too well earlier on and now we are going to suffer."

The opening batsman took guard. A few seconds later, his off stump virtually impaled the wicket keeper's stomach as he was bowled first ball and I dropped myself down to No. 4. The man I sent in instead went to the wicket looking distinctly green and again trudged back after just one ball, in a state of deep shock. I dropped myself down to No. 5!

The same scenario was repeated. At this point I decided that the captain should show some guts and I walked out to face the inevitable.

On my way to the wicket I passed John Snow, whom I knew slightly. "Hi, Snowy," I called out. "How nice to see you again. You must let me buy you a drink after the game." With a nervous laugh, I then nodded in the direction of the shell-shocked departing batsman and added pleadingly: "You're not going to do that to me as well are you? "

"Parky (Jim Parks) says that we might let you off the hook when you are 10 for 7," replied Snowy, marching back to start his full Test match run up.

I decided there was only one way to deal with this and that was to hit him off his length. As he came charging in, I waited until he was in his last stride and then advanced two paces down the wicket. And as his arm came over I closed my eyes, swung the bat and played probably the best cover drive of my entire cricketing career. I opened my eyes in time to see the ball streak over the boundary. What with my advance down the wicket and the sheer momentum of Snowy's follow-through, we ended up standing virtually face-to-face. All I could think of to say was: "I'm terribly, terribly sorry."

He said nothing, but simply glowered and stalked back to his mark. It seemed to take an age for him to get there. He turned and launched himself into an even more energetic run-up. This time, as his arm came over, I stepped back, raised by bat high about my shoulders and allowed the 80 mph delivery to shatter my stumps.

At the end of the day everyone was happy. Jim Parks had had a good collection. The crowd had been well entertained. The players had been wined and dined. And we had mingled with the stars.

Afterwards, we all retired to The Plough for a very convivial evening during which I was able to help one particular member of the opposition with a delicate problem. Once again, I had better not identify him. Suffice it to say that he was one of Sussex's more charismatic England Test stars – very charming, extremely good-looking, six-foot-four and every inch a ladies' man.

Before going down to the pub, he took me on one side and asked me if I would mind looking after his beautiful, blonde girlfriend for a short time. He explained that he had double dated by mistake and had to go and meet his other girlfriend off the train at Brighton station. His plan was for me to take girlfriend No 1 to the pub and keep her talking on the far side of the main bar while he would fetch girlfriend No 2 and take her into the other bar. From then on, he said, he would play it by ear!

I couldn't quite see how he was going to be able to pull this off but, sure enough, he somehow managed to keep the two of them apart and flitted backwards and forwards between the two bars. He kept this up successfully for about an hour until a third girlfriend, yet another stunningly attractive blonde, suddenly arrived in the pub, rushed straight up to him and threw her arms around his neck with a cry of: "Sorry I'm late, darling."

Exit one flustered cricketer, comprehensively caught and bowled!

During my time as captain of Rottingdean, we did briefly have one ex-Sussex county player in the team. We were gathered in The Plough one Friday evening in April, discussing the forthcoming season's fixtures, team selections, batting orders and so on, when Jack Goss asked: "Have you heard about Bob Pountain?"

"No," I said. "What about him?"

Bob was an opening bat for Sussex in the 1960's. He matched the famously big-hitting Colin Milburn in girth and also had Colin's wonderful eye for the ball. He was a fast-scoring opener, very exciting to watch. His weight, however, was a problem. It concerned the county so much that they suggested he should slim down a bit.

I understand that his immediate reaction was to tell them to f*** off. Their response was to tell him to do the same.

"I bumped into him the other days and suggested that he might like to play for us," said Jack. "He was up for it. What do you think?"

"Great," I said. "Let's play him on Sunday and see how it all works out."

Bob presented himself at the pavilion on Sunday. He was even larger than I remembered him in his Sussex days, but appeared to be very amiable. He also had a very bad stutter.

We fielded first and I put Bob in the slips. After about four overs

I then decided to make several field changes, one of which involved him.

"Would you mind moving to gully, Bob," I said.

"I'll st-st-stay here, th-th-thank you sk-sk-skipper," came the reply.

"No, Bob. I want you in the gully, please."

"I'll f-f-fucking st-st-stay here, skip," he insisted.

At this point I apologised to the batsmen and explained: "We seem to be having a little local difficulty here, but until this chap does as requested I'm afraid we are not going to be able to proceed."

In the end, he reluctantly agreed to move, but other problems arose during the match. And that wasn't all. Having downed about four pints in The Plough afterwards, Bob announced that he rather fancied one of the barmaids and was going to chat her up.

I advised strongly against this course of action, warning him: "It will all end in tears."

I was told in no uncertain terms that it was none of my business. "Anyway, what's the problem?" he added.

"Well, I am just trying to be helpful, Bob. There are three very good reasons why you shouldn't."

"Oh yeah? What are they, then?" he asked, draining his pint.

"Well, firstly she is only sixteen. Secondly, she is the landlord's daughter and he will murder you if you so much as look at her the wrong way. And thirdly, she is, by all accounts, a lesbian."

"In that case," he said, "I'll have another pint instead."

As time passed, I realised I could not captain him and he left the team. Then, three months later, we were playing at a lovely ground in Haywards Heath against a very strong side. We elected to bat first and as they took to the field I noticed a familiar, bulky figure taking up position in the slips.

The first wicket fell and I went in to bat. After taking my guard, I took a look around the field and when my gaze moved to the slip cordon I said amiably: "Hi Bob. Nice to see you again. What are you doing here?"

He fixed me with a baleful stare and said in a very loud voice that must have been heard not just by every one of his team-mates on the pitch but by the two hundred spectators as well: "It's all b-b-because of you, sk-sk-skip, that I'm p-p-playing for this b-b-bloody awful s-s-side."

One of the most entertaining benefit matches I was involved in was on behalf of John Edrich. I captained a celebrity side against his XI and among the stars who turned out were Eric Morecambe and Ernie Wise, Michael Parkinson and the actor Tom Baker, who was playing Dr Who at the time. He fielded wearing his long Dr Who scarf and children kept running up to him on the pitch. He would hoist them onto his shoulders to carry them back to their mothers and the expression on these kids' faces as he did so was absolutely marvellous.

I knew nothing about him as a cricketer and I was amazed when I decided to give him an over or two, just to please the crowd, to discover that he was a magnificent medium/fast bowler. In fact, he was so good that he took four wickets in his first two overs and I had to take him off in order to keep the game alive.

Not quite so impressive was the performance of newscaster McDonald Hobley. I remember playing with him in another celebrity game that was staged in the grounds of a stately home. The hospitality was very good on this occasion. We were batting second – after a very good lunch – and as 'Mac' waited to go in, well down the order, he continued to refresh himself. Suddenly, when another wicket fell and he was the next man in, we realised that he was missing. A frantic search ended when we found him happily floating around on his back in the swimming pool, fully dressed in his cricketing gear, including his pads, and with a glass still in his hand. He was completely pissed.

If the date July 31st, 1966 rings a bell in your mind it's probably because that was the day England won the World Cup. Unfortunately, when compiling our fixture list months before, we had overlooked the fact that the final was due to be played that Saturday and had arranged a match against a rival village team. At least 75% of both teams would undoubtedly have preferred to be watching the football.

My popularity soared when I arrived at the pavilion with a portable television, pretty rare in those days. I then managed to win the toss and immediately elected to bat first so that we could watch the match while we weren't actually at the crease. The only problem seemed to be ensuring that my batsmen did not throw their wickets away just so they could return to the pavilion.

Things appeared to be working out perfectly as I declared our innings at tea, with just fifteen minutes to go at Wembley before the final whistle was due to blow at the end of ninety minutes. But we'd reckoned without the Germans' last-minute equaliser and the need for extra time!

This meant we would now have to take to the field just as the match was reaching a nail-biting climax.

I had a chat with the opposition skipper and suggested that we should extend the tea interval by half-an-hour, so that we could all watch the match.

"No problem," he said.

I went up to Jack Beck and the other umpire. Jack was the gardener at St Aubyn's, my old preparatory school in Rottingdean, and delighted in telling anybody who cared to listen that I had been 'a sad little sod' ever since the age of eight. He was also a dyed-in-the-wool rugby man who regarded soccer as a game for cissies.

"Rules are rules," intoned Jack, refusing to extend close-of-play from 6.30pm to 7.00pm to make up for the lost half-an-hour.

And so it was that I had to lead my lot out onto the field and missed the climax to the greatest football final ever, listening in frustration to the roars of triumph that echoed from the pavilion as Geoff Hurst scored England's winning goals.

# IX

# A CAPITAL ADVENTURE

I N MANY WAYS, that World Cup victory of 1966 marked the highpoint of the Swinging Sixties. Our footballers, like our pop stars, ruled the world, London was hailed as its most fashionable and exciting capital and there was a general air of unbridled optimism, along with an exciting mood for change. Nowhere was this more clearly reflected than in the world of broadcasting, where the advent of Radio 1 in 1967 ushered in a new era. And just as I had nearly been in at the birth of commercial television in the late fifties and early sixties, I soon found myself at the very heart of the radio revolution that was taking place a decade later. Only this time it came about quite by chance.

After eleven happy and successful years with Southern Television, I left in 1969 to set up on my own as an independent marketing consultant. My early clients included the shipping line Union Castle, which was interested in looking into the possibility of getting involved in local commercial radio in the south of England. As a result of my efforts on Union Castle's behalf I became very well versed in the details of the process whereby the Independent Broadcasting Authority was to distribute the various franchises.

Some time later, I was chatting to my good friend John Vogt, of Vogt Gliddon Advertising, when he happened to mention that his partner, Mike Gliddon, was to be a director of Network Broadcasting, a consortium that was hoping to get the entertainment franchise for London. I pointed out to John that Mike was actually ineligible to be a director, as an advertising agency's direct involvement was not permissible under the rules laid down by the IBA.

The end result of this was that Mike introduced me to Network's managing director, Neil Ffrench-Blake, who suggested I might like to join them as his deputy, in Mike's place. This was subject to the approval of Lord Ted Willis, the scriptwriter and creator of *Mrs Dale's Diary* and *Dixon of Dock Green*, who was heading the consortium.

I duly went to meet Lord Willis for tea in the House of Lords. He immediately suggested that I call him 'Ted' and said: "I've been asking a few people about you and they were all very complimentary. However, as they were all friends and associates of yours that was to be expected. Now, since you are obviously not perfect, what do you consider to be your major fault?"

I don't know why, but I replied without hesitation: "Well, I'm very good with other people's money, but hopeless with my own."

The second half of this statement was certainly true. Even when I decided to sell my house in the early seventies I managed to get my timing wrong and missed out on a fortune.

Purchasing a large listed house in Ebury Street, on the fringes of Belgravia, seemed at first like a very good move, especially when a circular from a local estate agent dropped through the letterbox asking householders in the area if they would be interested in renting out their properties. I would normally bin such leaflets straightaway, but on this occasion, for some reason, I telephoned the agent simply to say I wasn't interested.

The gentleman on the other end of the line said I might reconsider when he told me who the clients might be. I said I doubted that, but carry on. "Arabs" he said.

"Come round and have a drink," I said quickly.

He did, and told me there was an Arab family of five who wanted a let for two weeks and would pay £1,000 a week.

"Cash?"

"Yes!"

"Done".

I began to panic. What on earth had I done? Where was I going to live for two weeks? How would I get paid and when? Will the house be kept clean? Will they leave or become squatters? How do I keep an eye on them? What will the neighbours say?

Alarming stories of incidents that had occurred in houses that had been rented to Arabs were beginning to circulate. One that I had heard involved a servant's unfamiliarity with a lavatory, having been accustomed back home to using a desert stone to do the necessary. When someone had politely explained the function of loo paper he quickly grasped the point and having collected a number of stones from the garden, had wrapped the lavatory paper around them!

As it turned out, any fears I might have had proved unfounded. I had been told by the estate agent that they would hand over the rent in advance and in cash. A meeting was arranged in the Rib Room bar of the Carlton Tower Hotel and, just when I was beginning to panic, an emissary arrived with £2,000 in £5 notes stuffed into a Harrods carrier bag. They left on the due date and the house was in perfect condition. The only thing they did, and I gather this was quite usual, was to take all the mattresses from the bedrooms and lay them out on the floor in the drawing room where they all slept and, apparently, also ate.

My next door neighbours at the time were an aristocratic couple. Not the most considerate of neighbours, they gave lots of dinner parties in the summer in their back garden and one morning after a particularly uproarious soiree I found an empty bottle of champagne in my garden, which had obviously been flung over my wall. I retaliated a few days later by chucking over an empty bottle of brown ale!

The news that I had let my house to Arabs circulated fast and it soon came back to me that they thought I had behaved disgracefully and that I was letting down the social tone of the district. However, soon after my tenants had departed, a convoy of Rolls Royces drew up outside, next door, and disgorged at least a dozen Arab men and women. I later heard that they were paying over £2,000 per week. The only difference between our two houses was that their furniture mostly came from Blenheim Palace!

As it happens, I never did rent it out again. Eventually the house proved to be too large for my needs and in 1976 I sold it for £75,000. A few months later the property market took off with a vengeance and not that long afterwards I was sickened to notice that the house had been put up for sale at £1,000,000!

Anyway, my admission of incompetence when it came to matters of personal finance seemed to go down well with Ted Willis and we retired to the bar to seal the start of a most enjoyable association and friendship.

Other members of the consortium's board of directors included Ned Sherrin, Sylvia Peters, Oxford professor of broadcasting Tony Smith and Janet Fookes, MP. Plus, of course, the obligatory merchant banker, Neil Ffrench-Blake, a former broadcaster and BBC executive who had put the group together. An Old Etonian, married to the daughter of the Duke of St. Albans, Neil was not only very well connected but also extremely creative – and he never took 'No' for an answer.

He had found some very nice offices in South Audley Street through his connections with Colonel Stirling, one of the founders of the SAS who had offices in the same building. We moved in and set about preparing our bid for what was, undoubtedly, the biggest prize in broadcasting outside the major commercial television franchises. The London 'entertainment' station would be the largest radio station in the UK and potentially the most profitable. There was also to be a London based news station, which went to LBC.

We had a pretty good idea of our opposition. With nine months to go before the December 1972 deadline for applications to be received by the IBA there were effectively eight runners and riders, among them a consortium called Capital Radio. This was headed by Lord Attenborough and included a number of high profile show business names such as Brian Forbes, George Martin and David Jacobs. We were perpetually analysing all the available information about our rivals in order to assess the threat they posed and I have to say that, at this stage, Capital were way down the list. We understood they had no senior management in place, no newspaper association – which was a compulsory IBA requirement – and no known financial structure.

We, on the other hand, were in reasonably good shape. We had the finance, we had key executives lined up and we had a newspaper tie-up. A programme format was being created that involved broadcasting twenty-four hours a day, right from the start. That was something that had never been attempted in this country before, in either television or radio.

In addition, we already had studio premises lined up in St. Martins Lane, above the advertising agency Leo Burnett. Our financial director had negotiated very favourable terms for the lease of this property, mainly because his father, a very successful property developer, was the owner! With room for over one hundred staff, as well as the studios themselves, the place was perfect for our requirements. It also had the additional asset of a prime West End location. Conveniently close to Whitehall and the Houses of Parliament, it provided easy assess for politicians involved in studio interviews and was even handier for theatreland and the showbiz fraternity.

With Professor Tony Smith masterminding the programme schedule, Robin Marmor overseeing the financial structure, former Fleet Street news editor James Anderson looking after the Press and publicity requirements, Robin D'eath in charge of the engineering side and me taking responsibility for advertising sales, we reckoned we had a pretty strong team.

As around 95% of commercial radio income derived from advertising income, this was obviously a critical part of the company's structure. Our first task was to create a sales department and produce a rate card that would impress both national and local advertisers. We also needed a so-called 'traffic' department, for the administration of commercials through from sale to transmission, and a clearance procedure for approving advertisements before they went out on air.

When it comes to hiring staff, I have always been a firm believer in nepotism. Better the devil you know! In that respect, poaching the best people from a company you have recently left is always a particularly good option and I wasted no time in pinching a senior sales executive from Southern to become our Advertising Sales Director. The employment of charismatic, extroverted, good-looking people – especially women – also pays dividends in my experience.

One obvious problem we faced in recruiting people in advance of winning the franchise was that they had to be sounded out in conditions of utmost secrecy, since those in senior positions elsewhere could not afford to let their existing employers know that they were thinking of defecting. The BBC and the ITV companies, in particular, had threatened dire consequences for anyone found to be in negotiation with a consortium. In fact, our chief engineer, who was employed by ATV when we approached him, was found out and was banished to the Epilogue for six months, a punishment that was likened to being sent to Siberia.

What made all this a real Catch 22 situation was that the IBA were demanding to know who the various consortia had got lined up as senior executives, in order to help them make their decision as to which were the strongest and most suitable applicants. Many of the interviews I set up had therefore to be conducted clandestinely in my Ebury Street house, out of office hours. You could not possibly lunch in a public place, because in the world of advertising and the media everybody knows everybody else, gossip is rife and the chances were that your bosses would know where you'd been and exactly whom you had been seeing before you got back to the office.

At the same time, the wining and dining of certain influential contacts could not be undertaken without considerable expenditure on entertaining. The likes of MPs, union bosses, bankers and key showbiz figures had to be cultivated assiduously and, let's face it, you can't take those sort of people to the equivalent of Joe's Snack Bar. It was important for us to be able to undertake this vital work without some hard-nosed, faceless, humourless and probably jealous accountant querying every lunch and dinner bill. Luckily, at Network we had no such 'party pooper', so I was able to start on a hectic schedule of entertaining. Dirty work, but somebody's got to do it!

In fact, we were all working round-the-clock in the hectic months leading up to December 3rd, 1972, when all forty-five consortia involved in bidding for franchises around the country had to deliver their applications to the IBA. Apart from a general mission statement, these applications had to include detailed information about the members of the board, the names of the senior management (in strictest confidence, if necessary), a sample programme format, a three-year business plan of projected income and expenditure, full technical data and details about planned studio facilities.

As the deadline for the delivery of our application to the IBA in Brompton Road approached, there was a last-minute panic when severe flooding in the area around our printer's premises in Dorset threatened to put them temporarily out of action. The consequences of not having our prospectus printed and bound in time would have been disastrous. Luckily, however, the waters subsided at the eleventh hour and all was well.

At this stage we felt very confident. We satisfied all the basic criteria and, on top of everything else, we had invested a huge amount of extra time, effort and money into researching and planning how to provide a service that would appeal broadly to all Londoners. Obviously we wanted the IBA to know how determined we were to gauge the general consensus before deciding on our programming content outside the general music format. To this end, Lord Willis had personally hosted a series of lunches at which a selection of twelve special guests would be invited to express their opinions about London as a capital city. Is it a simple north/south divide, or a series of villages, each with their own identity? What most represents London in people's minds – Pigeons? Guardsmen? Double-decker buses? All the people we consulted were household names from every walk of life, ranging from Bruce Forsyth and footballer Danny Blanchflower to Mervyn Stockwood, the Bishop of Southwark.

Once the applications had been considered, short-listed candidates were to be summoned for interview in January 1973. This was the bit I was not looking forward to. I have never been the most confident public speaker and the thought of having to get up in front of the IBA and do my bit to convince them that we were worthy of being awarded the coveted licence to broadcast filled me with dread. I likened it to an actor's first night nerves. But all the actor has to worry about is learning his lines, hitting his mark and making sure he is familiar with the set. In our case, we had a rough idea of the questions that were likely to be asked and had carefully rehearsed the answers. But we also knew that we were certain to be hit with one or two surprises.

It was only when the other short-listed interview candidates were announced that we began to suspect that Capital, far from being a rank outsider, were a real threat. Even so, we remained extremely optimistic.

There was little more to do until the interview, which was scheduled for 9.00am and would last ninety minutes. Applicants were told that they could 'field' whoever they wanted, but that the IBA would obviously want to question the heads of each department.

With the media camped outside in force, trying to interview and photograph all the comings and goings throughout the day, complex arrangements had been made to try and protect those who still didn't want to be publicly identified because of their existing jobs. It was also important to ensure that one group of applicants did not clash with another when arriving or leaving.

To this end, arrangements were made to have 'private' visitors smuggled in via a back entrance, while different waiting rooms were provided for overlapping applicants. Needless to say, the supposedly 'secret' back entrance didn't fool the more enterprising journalists, who were lurking there with their cameramen.

Our team – Ted Willis, Neil Ffrench-Blake, Ned Sherrin, Professor Tony Smith, our merchant banker and I – had got together the day before for a final rehearsal. Ted stayed overnight in the Hyde Park Hotel, adjacent to the IBA, while Neil Ffrench-Blake retired to the Knightsbridge Casino, where he usually reported when the pressure was on!

We reassembled at 8.30am the next morning, all of us, except Ted and Ned, in a very nervous condition. Before we were ushered into the presence of the full membership of the Independent Broadcasting Authority, Ted rendered a rallying call by reciting Henry V's 'Once more into the breach'!

The interview room was enormous, with the members of the Authority seated at a semi-circular table and the various officers of the IBA ranged behind them. These officers were not allowed to talk but passed notes to their masters. There were two stenographers sitting opposite each other in the middle, silently typing every word. Our team, at the opposite end, sat down with a cigarette box and lighter in front of each of us.

After we had been formally welcomed by Lord Aylestone, the chairman of the IBA, I went to take a cigarette and suddenly realised it was impossible. My hand was shaking so much it would have looked pathetic.

As each question was asked by a member of the Authority, Ted Willis would field it and ask for the relevant member of our team to respond.

Lady Sharpe, a pleasant but nevertheless rather frightening personality, asked if we could explain why our advertising forecasts were so optimistic compared with those of some of our rivals. Ted Willis indicated that this was one for me to answer.

I had just started to explain (very lucidly I thought) when the IBA's Head of Radio, John Thompson, who was sitting immediately behind Lord Alyestone, started scribbling furiously. I was convinced he was going to pass a note to the Chairman saying, in effect, that I was talking a load of nonsense. Starting to panic, I immediately dried up and only managed with great difficulty to get back into my stride.

Many weeks after this, I was lunching with John Thompson and referred to this incident. He immediately recalled the moment, explaining: "As you were talking, I suddenly remembered that my wife had told me when I left the house that morning that on no account must I forget to purchase some kippers on my way home. So I made a note of it."

It was on that sort of episode that a licence to broadcast could have been won or lost!

Overall, we reckoned things had gone pretty well and we were confident we would have done better than Capital, whose team were to follow us later in the day. It therefore came as a bit of a shock when, two days later, we were informed that the IBA liked "elements of both of us" and asked us to get together to see if we could submit a combined application, all the other applicants having been ruled out.

We immediately held a board meeting to decide how our chairman, Ted Willis, should approach a meeting with Capital's Richard Attenborough. Our discussions centred on what we considered to be our respective strengths and weaknesses.

We had assumed that one of the things that would count most heavily against Capital was the fact that they had not identified any of the senior executives who would be running the station. It turned out, however, that Richard Attenborough had come up with a very good response when this was raised during the IBA interview. He admitted that they had no specific people in mind, adding that he and his board had come to the conclusion that it would be morally wrong to go behind the backs of the BBC and the commercial television companies in an effort to 'lock in' certain individuals on the basis that Capital *might* be awarded the licence, since this would put the individuals concerned at risk of losing their current employment without any guarantee that there would be a job at Capital for them to go to. Instead, he invited the IBA themselves to suggest whom they thought should be considered for the various senior management posts.

The logic behind this bold suggestion was that as the IBA had studied all the applications and knew everybody associated with them, including those who had asked not to be publicly identified, they were in a better position than anyone to know who might be available and who would be best qualified and have most to offer.

We appreciated that this was a very clever response, putting that particular ball very firmly in the IBA's court, while showing Capital in a favourable light as being open-minded in their commitment to get the best people for the jobs. We also accepted that they did have some pretty solid and respected names on their board. However, we also knew that they had no money and also that they had a problem with their newspaper interest. We, on the other hand, had the staff, the money, the studios and the newspaper involvement, but were aware that our financial structure was somewhat shaky. In that area we believed we could quickly readdress any concerns by bolstering our merchant banker's interest, albeit at the eleventh hour.

It was eventually agreed that Ted Willis should meet Richard Attenborough with the proposal for a 'merger' that would give Capital 40% and Network 60%. The meeting took place and Ted reported back that no agreement could be reached as Capital were intent on 'going for broke'. Not even a 50/50 split was deemed feasible since this would almost inevitably end up as a buggers' muddle.

When we reported back that we couldn't reach an agreement, the IBA then decided that both teams must be reinterviewed. Again, we put up what we thought was a more than adequate performance, although our new financial structure did look very much like a panic measure. However, we were still about 80% confident that we had the edge. The day before the IBA were to announce their decision the *Evening Standard*'s front page headline was: '*Ted Willis Favourite to Win London Radio Franchise*'.

This was heady stuff and we all slept well. But at 6.30am I was called by Ted Willis, who said he was about to get into his bath and drown himself as the IBA had informed him that Capital were to be awarded the London Entertainment Radio Licence and that we were to get absolutely nothing.

This was devastating news and there was not only disappointment but also bitterness in certain quarters that the prize had gone to a consortium who, it was felt, had not properly adhered to the IBA's specifications for applicants.

However, Richard Attenborough stood by his avowed intention to seek the views of the IBA in filling Capital's senior posts. As I had suspected might be the case, based on this criteria, John Whitney was appointed Managing Director. Along with MP John Gorst, he had been a driving force behind the Local Radio Association, which had successfully lobbied Parliament to pass the Bill that legalised commercial radio.

Having myself established an amiable relationship with many of the people at the IBA over the years – and given my involvement with Network – I dared to hope that my name might also be mentioned favourably at some stage. Sure enough, in the first week of April 1973, Richard Attenborough phoned to ask if he could call on me at my home in Ebury Street.

On arrival, he indicated that the company were interested in whether I might join Capital either as Sales Director or General Manager. Obviously I was delighted and said that I would prefer the position of General Manager as I especially enjoyed administration. I felt that as a salesman I always had the problem of seeing the other person's point of view (a fatal flaw!). So, General Manager it was.

I started work the very next day. At this stage we were working out of Richard Attenborough's personal office in Park Lane, right next door to the Dorchester Hotel, and the entire staff consisted of John Whitney and myself, John's secretary Jo Wilding, my secretary, Melanie, an excellent Australian lady, and the Chairman's wonderfully efficient PA, Jackie. We had no Programme Controller or Advertising Sales department and no studio. We didn't even have a proper office of our own. And we were due to go on air in twenty-four weeks' time on October 16th, 1973! LBC were to launch a week earlier on the 8th, the IBA having decided that, as the news station, they were a more 'serious' broadcaster than Capital as the entertainment station.

After a few days, Jackie mentioned that she had spotted some empty premises in Piccadilly that she thought might make a suitable office. Together, we went round to have a look. Virtually next door to the Naval and Military Club – known as the 'In and Out' – the place had previously been a Jaguar car showroom, with a reception area facing the street. Behind this, on the ground floor, was a large open space, which had been the actual showroom. There was also a basement, which I recognised as having once been the site of The Carousel, one of London's most famous nightclubs back in the fifties, when I had spent many a happy evening there. We eventually tracked down the 'caretaker', a rough, bearded and short-tempered man who actually turned out to be much more than a caretaker and was able to discuss and negotiate terms. We agreed, there and then, on a six-month lease with immediate occupancy.

There then ensued a period of frantic and often chaotic activity during which this empty shell of a building was transformed into a functioning office. The first priority was to install a telephone switchboard and plenty of extensions, along with a receptionist to operate the system. At the same time, we had to plan the main open area in such a way that the various departments were separated from one another by lines of potted plants. The lighting and heating had to be sorted out. Office furniture and stationery had to be ordered – everything from desks, chairs, filing cabinets, cupboards, typewriters and copying machines right down to pens, pencils and paper. And, of course, tea and coffee-making facilities had to be provided, not to mention a drinks cabinet for the General Manager!

Suitable locations also had to be found for a boardroom, a conference room and offices for the Chairman and Managing Director. As far as the latter were concerned, there was a mezzanine area at one end of the open-plan office that was similar to a ship's bridge, ideal to set the Chairman and Managing Director apart in the privacy they required.

There was a side entrance to the building that led out to Shepherds Market, which was well provided with restaurants, pubs, and coffee bars. Bearing in mind that many of us were regularly working for up to eighteen hours a day, these were very welcome facilities.

It was against this background of semi-organised chaos that John and I were trying to get on with the serious business of getting the station up and running, and it wasn't long before we hit our first major crisis.

As Programme Controller, we had recruited a woman who, although English, had been running Washington D.C's non-commercial information television channel. Her appointment had been announced to the media and given prominent coverage in *Broadcast*, the main media trade journal. Unfortunately, this lady proceeded to give a full interview to *Broadcast* in which she expressed aims and intentions that were completely contrary to the overall programming policy of Capital, as submitted in their application.

The situation escalated so quickly and so harmfully that we were left with no other option but to fly her over to London, where she was met at Heathrow and her appointment revoked before she had even left the terminal.

We now lost another vital few weeks as we searched for a replacement. In the meantime, we still had no Programme Department heads, no programme format and no disc jockeys. The man we eventually appointed as Programme Controller was Michael Bukht, later to become better known as Michael Barry, the 'Crafty Cook' on Capital and a regular presenter on BBC TV's *Food & Drink*. With just sixteen weeks to go to the launch, we now had at least the beginnings of a programming department, including a Head of Music and a Chief Engineer. We also had an Advertising Sales Director, Tony Vickers, and a Financial Director, Robin Fletcher.

As the deadline for our on-air debut approached at an alarming rate, and amid continuing pandemonium, the pressure was ratcheted up day-by-day and there were many times when I awoke in the wee small hours before dawn in a cold sweat of panic. Our Chairman, however, remained a tower of strength, always cool in a crisis.

Dickie Attenborough's achievements as a film director, producer and actor have been well chronicled and the plaudits he has received are fully deserved. His exceptional all-round ability in the world of film and show business is unsurpassed. What may not be so widely appreciated is his acute business sense and ability to go to the heart of the problem without hesitation. His memory recall and aptitude to switch from one subject to another is sometimes quite unnerving.

I remember one occasion when we were going through a particularly thin time at Capital and I had once again gone to see Dickie to discuss various mundane aspects of general administration, including the idea of cutting our spiralling costs by reducing the number of Xerox copying machines.

At that time he was in the throes of trying to put together the film *Ghandi*, which was an obsession and a very personal crusade. As we were talking, the telephone rang. It was a call from America and for the next ninety minutes I sat enthralled. The conversation ranged over the raising of a budget of millions of pounds, the employment of thousands of extras, the provision of transport and accommodation across the Indian continent and the need to keep to a strict production schedule that would ensure the film was completed by a certain date in order to qualify for Oscar nominations.

At the end of the ninety minutes, one would have expected any normal mortal to sink his head in his hands and ask to be left alone while he gathered his thoughts. But not Dickie! He calmly replaced the receiver and, without pausing for even a second said: "Now, Tony, about those Xerox machines..."

He was a man who would not easily allow anything to cramp his style. The large, curved, sweeping staircase in the foyer at the entrance to the Capital Radio studios at Euston Tower has always been an imposing and impressive feature to every visitor. We were strapped for cash when building the studio complex there in the months leading up to the launch and the quote for the staircase was exceptionally high compared with all the other work.

Picking my moment during a relaxed conversation with Dickie, I mentioned that I thought the cost of the staircase was somewhat exorbitant and that it must surely make sense if we could save thousands of pounds by going for a cheaper design.

"But darling," cried Dickie. "Can't you just imagine Anna Neagle sweeping down those stairs in her evening dress?"

I could and did. As usual, he was absolutely right.

It was much the same with the design of the Capital logo. This seemed a pretty simple and straightforward matter to me and I proposed that our regular advertising agency should be asked to come up with some ideas.

"No, no," said Dickie. "This must be undertaken by Pentagram. They are the best logo specialists in the country."

Representatives from Pentagram duly arrived and asked for our general views on the key messages that we wanted to put across and then went away. A week later they came back with their presentation.

What they had come up with was very nice. The lettering of the word 'Capital' was good and there was a dove/pigeon with a musical note emitting from its mouth.

The design was put out for everyone to see and opinions sought.

"Very nice," I said. "I expect the alternatives will be just as interesting."

"Alternatives, darling?" replied Dickie. "Pentagram don't do alternatives. That's it."

I realised I had entered a world of which I had no experience. Apparently, one committed oneself, at a huge and previously agreed price, to a once-and-for-all proposal. I still don't accept the premise, but I bow to the judgement of my experienced betters.

It was, and still is, a great logo!

Despite the nerve-wracking build-up, our launch went ahead right on schedule at 5.30am on October 16th. Almost until the very last moment I was convinced that it might not happen. Apart from anything else, the studio complex at Euston had only been finished two weeks beforehand!

Inevitably, there were teething troubles – some of them quite serious, others amusing and one or two a bit of both. For instance, just prior to the launch we had obtained from the States a fancy machine that enabled commercials to be automatically loaded, timed and transmitted throughout the day at the times booked by the advertiser.

Unfortunately, during the first hour of broadcasting the machine went berserk and pumped out sixteen minutes of advertisements when the strict IBA regulations permitted no more than nine. We immediately discarded the stupid thing and went manual. However, this entailed union problems, as the duty engineers claimed it was not part of their job simply to push a little advertisement cartridge into a machine from time to time. As a result, we had to employ six women, rostered over twenty-four hours, seven days a week, to slot in the advertisement cartridges at the required times.

This was a ridiculous financial burden for the company, when a negotiable payment to the duty engineers could have resolved the problem. But these were the days of Alan Sapper, the notorious General Secretary of the ACCT. Creating extra union jobs was part of their policy. The advertisements were our lifeblood, so we couldn't afford to argue and the women were brought in simply to do this effortless and mind-numbingly boring job.

One of these ladies, I soon noticed, seemed to be particularly popular and it wasn't too hard to see why. Busty and attractive, she also had a very extrovert personality and was always smiling at everyone. As soon as she arrived, an abnormally large number of engineers started volunteering for night shifts at times when she was on duty. I had no problem with that – a happy work force was just what you wanted. Unfortunately, she obviously found the attention of the men as distracting as they found her and she started to miss the times when she should have been inserting the commercials.

Because of the nature of their job, the women had been nick-named "stuffers" and, right from the start, this one lived up to her name with enthusiasm. I knew I had to dispense with her services, but I was aware of the union implications if I were to give the real reason for her dismissal.

I summoned her to a meeting, during which the conversation went roughly as follows:

"I'm sorry, Jane, but things don't seem to be working out too well."

"Oh! Why is that?"

"Well, on several occasions you've missed the time slot for putting out the commercials."

"That's not the problem. I know why you're going to fire me."

"You do?" I asked, somewhat apprehensively.

"Yes!" she cried. "It's because I'm a nymphomaniac."

"Good God! You? A nymphomaniac? Well, I'd never have believed that. But no, no no. It's only that your work hasn't been up to standard."

She beamed a huge smile. "It's OK," she said. "No hard feelings. I am a nymphomaniac and I have enjoyed my time here. Goodbye and good luck".

One Sunday lunchtime about six months later I was in my local pub with a few friends when I suddenly noticed Jane at the far end of the bar. She spotted me at the same moment and, bursting out of her Capital Radio T-shirt, shouted across to her friends: "Look over there – that's the bloke who sacked me for being a nymphomaniac!"

It seemed as if every unaccompanied man in the pub suddenly had a very good reason to sidle round to her side of the bar.

One of the first regular late evening programmes we broadcast was presented by Marsha Hunt, perhaps most famous for having had a love child by Mick Jagger. It was a chat show that featured a number of well-known guests sitting around a table reminiscing about their past. On one occasion her guests included Simon Raven, 'M' from James Bond and photographer Lord Lichfield.

For once, I was not working late and went to bed at 10.00pm, listening to the programme. I could hear the distinctive clink of glasses onto wine bottles and it was clear from their tone of voice that this particular group of guests had enjoyed a considerable amount of 'hospitality'.

Matters seemed to be getting somewhat out of control when one of the guests announced his dislike of a particularly famous London food emporium and tea shop, especially its cake counter, which he had visited earlier that day. What had upset him, he said, was that the male sales staff seemed to be 'queer'.

"Well, why didn't you report it to the manager?" asked Marsha.

"I couldn't" he said. "He was bloody queer as well".

At this point I started to become rather nervous and apprehensive, foreseeing a call from this highly prestigious establishment the next day complaining that Capital Radio had damaged their image and threatening us with their lawyers.

However, I was quickly distracted when 'M' began to recount his meeting with an Italian film star.

"Who was that?" Marsha asked, as the wine glasses continued to clink.

"Gina Lollobrigida," slurred 'M'.

Another guest, who had already been asked by Marsha to stop putting his hand up her skirt, then interrupted this fascinating intellectual conversation and shouted:

"Marsha, your microphone's a very phallic shape. Why don't you suck it and give us a simulated orgasm?"

I leapt for the telephone, intent on instructing the producer to stop the show immediately and to play some music instead. This was not my direct responsibility, but I wasn't sure that the Programme Controller was listening or, indeed, even if he were, whether he would put a stop to it. My concern, of course, was the IBA, our masters, who had the power to revoke our licence.

It was impossible to get through. Obviously the whole of London was ringing to complain, I thought. In fact, the next morning I found that hundreds of calls had been recorded, 99% of which had congratulated Capital on an invigorating programme. The general view seemed to be that it had provided great entertainment and that more of the same would be very welcome.

Another very successful chat show during those early months was presented by Allan Hargreaves, whose guests on various occasions included the Chief Witch of England, the Head Satanist of Great Britain and Lord (Frank) Longford.

I met Lord Longford in our hospitality room prior to the programme and found out that he had been at Eton with my father in the 1920's. We had quite a long conversation during which he was able to tell me a little more about the father I had never really known and I found him altogether charming.

During the programme itself, his discussion with Allan became quite heated and ended with Allan challenging him to return the following week. He readily agreed to do so and they retired to the hospitality room. Later, Allan took me to one side to tell me that his Lordship had requested two cases of champagne as his fee for returning. He eventually agreed to settle for one case and then, to our surprise, asked if he could throw a small party for the programme staff with the champagne and made a point of asking Allan to bring along his attractive P.A!

It would have been interesting to see how Lord Longford might have got on with Linda Lovelace, who also visited Capital in 1974 to be interviewed. For those under the age of forty, it should be explained that Ms Lovelace was the top Hollywood porn star of the day, famed forever for her performance in the film *Deep Throat*, the title of which should leave little doubt about the subject matter. According to legend, she went into strict training before making the film!

Normally, there would only have been a small number of people still in the building at the time in the evening when this particular programme went out – the presenter, scheduled disc jockeys, producers, studio staff, duty engineers and the security man downstairs. But on this occasion it seemed that our entire staff of 120 all suddenly had pressing reasons for working late and it looked for a while as though the police would have to be called to control the staff inside rather than the crowd outside.

I, of course, put myself in charge of hospitality for the evening.

Meanwhile, the Unions were busy trying to make their presence felt. Those we had to deal with included the ACCT (Engineering), the NUJ (Journalists) and NATKE (Secretarial, Admin). Inevitably, the people involved in running the 'shops' (ACCT, NATKE) and the 'chapel' (NUJ) were inexperienced, as indeed were the management – none more so than myself. But as General Manager, I was the initial point of contact.

After a while I got to thinking that a little bit of team sport would be beneficial for all of us and might help us to 'bond' a little more, so I decided to arrange a cricket match. Liza Myers, my P.A., lived in Speldhurst, a delightful village in Kent, and so a match was organised against the local village side. I posted an invitation on the notice board asking anyone who wished to be selected to put their names forward. As it happened, eleven people responded, which should have made everything very simple.

But no!

That evening the Shop Steward of the ACCT asked to see me on a matter of some importance. I welcomed him into my office and poured him a drink. It was obvious he was somewhat embarrassed and he immediately apologised for bringing the matter up, but there had just been a shop meeting and he was obliged to see me and read out the relevant minute, as follows:

"We, the shop, deplore the fact that you, as General Manager, thought fit to select a cricket side for Capital Radio without any member of the Engineering Department being chosen."

They used to make Ealing comedies about this sort of thing, I thought to myself. After a second or two of dumbfounded silence, I reminded him that eleven people had put their names forward and that as a cricket team traditionally consisted of eleven players, those eleven had been selected..

He remarked, rather nervously, that this was irrelevant!

"Mike, may I go off the record?" I asked.

"Certainly," he replied, putting down his pen.

"You are a c***," I told him. "And your colleagues are c***s too."

The rather startled Shop Steward said nothing.

"Now, may I go back on the record?" I added.

"Of course," said Mike, picking up his pen with a slightly stunned look on his face.

"You are a c*** and your colleagues are c***s," I reiterated.

For a moment Mike looked totally shell-shocked and then a huge grin spread over his face, followed by a great bellow of laughter. I realised afterwards that I might well have ended up creating big problems for both myself and the company, but the stupidity of the situation had got the better of me.

It was all part of the teething problems that came up when a new industry was being created.

# X

## GOLDEN OLDIES

I T WAS SHORTLY before Capital went on air for the first time in 1973 that cricket fanatic Tim Rice, now Sir Tim, founded The Heartaches. The Heartaches is a truly unique cricket club. No fees are paid and membership is by the personal invitation of Tim himself. To be accorded this honour you have to be not only a reasonably competent player and a good team man, but also socially acceptable to Tim. This basically means that you have to be very polite to Tim at all times and show due appreciation of his bowling skills!

The fixtures, all arranged personally by Tim, are mainly against sides from the Home Counties but also include tours to Cornwall and even, occasionally, as far afield as the USA. The matches are played in a convivial spirit of intense but friendly rivalry and invariably take place at the most delightful venues, always with a good country pub very close at hand. In other words, this is amateur cricket at its traditional best.

I first met Tim at Capital when he became one of our early presenters, with a Sunday show in which in which he played selections of his favourite records. As General Manager, I was working seven days a week at that time and so it was inevitable that we should bump into each other in and around the studio. In fact, he was in and out of my office all the time, thanks entirely to the extra secretary I had had to get in to work for me at weekends. The agency sent along a young theatrical producer named Jane, who was 'resting' between jobs, a most attractive girl with a wonderful, bubbly personality. I was not at all surprised when she caught Tim's eye and they started to go out together – and absolutely delighted when they eventually got married.

Meanwhile, I was very pleased to be invited by Tim to play in a Heartaches match at a ground near his lovely home on the Oxfordshire/Gloucestershire border. It was a beautiful summer's day and we had a very good game. After everybody had retired to the local pub for a while, Tim then invited a few of us back to his house for dinner.

At the end of a splendid meal, we settled down in the drawing room to enjoy a brandy or two. It was a balmy summer evening, the French windows were open and, to quote P.G. Wodehouse, "all was well with the world".

This was at the time when Tim and Andrew Lloyd-Webber were working on *Evita*, which I believe was the first musical ever to be launched as an album before it opened on stage. The part of Evita was sung on the album by Julie Covington, who was staying at the house as one of Tim's weekend guests. As the brandy and liqueurs were being served, Tim suddenly asked if we would like to hear a run-through of the recording, which had just been completed in the studio but which nobody, not even Julie herself, had yet heard in its entirety.

What followed were moments to treasure forever as I became one of the first people privileged to enjoy an impromptu private preview of one of the greatest musicals in history, with the star herself sitting on the carpet, also listening to it for the first time. When it came to the song 'Don't Cry for Me, Argentina', there wasn't a dry eye in the room. It was just so moving, made even more so by Julie's reaction. She was genuinely quite overcome by the experience and that affected the rest of us.

I went on to have many more hugely enjoyable games with the Heartaches, but just before I could complete the fourteen that would entitle me to my 'colours', my stupid leg started to pack up and, with my mobility somewhat restricted, I had to stop playing.

Some two years later I mentioned to Tim how disappointed I was to have missed out, especially as I had played thirteen matches and had therefore fallen just one short of the required total.

"Well, the rules are very strict, you know, but I'll see what can be done," he said. True to his word, I got a call a week later from Eileen, the team Secretary.

"I know it's rather short notice, but are you by any chance available to turn out this Sunday?" she asked.

"I certainly am," I replied.

"Thank God for that," said Eileen. "We're one short and I've tried everyone else I can think of."

And so it was that I did get my coveted Heartaches colours before finally being forced, very sadly, to hang up my bat and pads for good. It is one of my great regrets that failing health prevented me from playing in more of their matches. They were always such fun.

Tim not only ran the whole thing with enormous enthusiasm, but also kept a detailed report of the team's performances over the years, which is contained in the annual Heartaches Cricketers' Almanac. A glance through the statistics at the back of the Almanac, probably the most detailed and varied provided by any club in the world, provides an extremely entertaining read. I include here a list of some of the headings to give a flavour of the club's colourful history.

Heartaches Top 5 Team Totals
Heartaches Bottom 5 Team Totals
Opponents Top 5 Team Totals
Opponents Bottom 5 Team Totals
Greatest Victories
Greatest Defeats
Longest Winning Sequence
Longest Undefeated Sequence
Longest Unvictorious Sequence
Longest Sequence of Draws
Tied Matches
Most Car Screen Windows Broken in One Match
　(*2 by Tom Graveney in 1983*)
Longest Heartaches Innings
Shortest Heartaches Innings
Heartaches Scoring Rate
Most Boring Scoring

All Time Extras Total
Batting Records
    Most Individual 50+ Records
    Most Individual 25+ records
    Highest Individual Score on Debut
    Batsmen Who Have Scored 1,000 runs
    Highest Average in a Season
    Most Runs in a Month
    Most Boundaries in an Innings
    Most Sixes in One Innings
    Highest Partnerships
    Distribution of Century Stands
    Record Partnership of Each Innings
Bowling
    Seven Wickets in an Innings
    Five Wickets in an Innings
    25 Wickets in a Season
    10 Wickets in a Season
    Bowlers who have Taken 100 Wickets
    Bowling Average of Less than 9 in a Season
    Most Overs Bowled in one Season by one Bowler
    Hat Tricks
Fielding
    Four catches in One Innings
    Three Catches in One Innings
    Seven Catches in One Season
    Fielders Who Have Held 30 Catches
Wicket Keeping
    Most Victims in a Career
    Most Victims in a Season
    Most Catches in a Season
    Most Stumpings in a Season

Wonderful stuff!

Although no longer able to play cricket, I continued to maintain an enthusiastic off-the-field interest in the game.

It was in my capacity as Hon. Sec. of Rottingdean C.C that I decided to try and spruce up the fixture card as a means of publicising the proud historic record of the club. To this end, I asked a number of well-known players and celebrities with whom I had been associated over the years if they would agree to be listed among 'The Friends of Rottingdean Cricket Club'.

All those I contacted were more than willing to lend their names. They included former England captains R.E.S. (Bob) Wyatt and Ted Dexter, former Sussex star, cricket journalist and Test selector Robin Marlar, comedian Leslie Crowther and Michael Aspel.

This success encouraged me to set my sights even higher. Unfortunately, in my excitement, I went right over the top and wrote off to the legendary Don Bradman, whom I had never met but had once seen playing when I was about eleven years old.

My letter was addressed to 'Sir Don' and referred to all the other well-known sportsmen and personalities who had kindly agreed to be 'Friends of Rottingdean', which, I explained, was one of the oldest cricket clubs in the world. Would he consider lending his name as well?

I really did not expect a reply, but four months later a letter arrived from Australia. I gently slit open the envelope with trembling fingers and pulled out the letter. The first thing I saw was the heading 'Sir Donald Bradman'. My little old heart was all of a flutter, even more so when I saw that it started in friendly fashion with 'Dear Tony'.

It went on:

"I received your correspondence, dated 19 October, asking me to become one of the 'Friends' of Rottingdean Cricket Club.

"As I am 77 and live 12,000 miles away it would be transparent to everybody that this would be nothing but a publicity gimmick and as such I think it would be more honest and sensible if I respectfully decline and leave tangible support for the Club to English residents who could conceivably have some association with the Club.

Yours faithfully, etc

Now, to some this might appear a little on the brusque side. But it has to be said that 'The Don' was quite right insofar as it most certainly was a publicity gimmick. And it was actually more than gracious of him to reply, enabling me to frame the letter and hang it over the bar in our pavilion. After all, how many cricket clubs in the U.K. have received a letter from the greatest cricketer of all time?

On reflection, I suspect that there could have been another very good reason for the rather abrupt tone of his response. I had added a P.S. to my letter, mentioning that he might be interested to know that Douglas Jardine was my Godfather and that I was also a good friend of R.E.S. (Bob) Wyatt. As Jardine was the England captain and Bob Wyatt his vice captain during the infamous bodyline tour of Australia in 1932/3, I have to admit that this was perhaps not the most tactful move! For non-cricket fans, bodyline was the tactic whereby fast bowler Harold Larwood was primed by his captain to aim intimidating bouncers straight at the batsman's body, the main target being Bradman himself, then at the peak of his powers.

By all accounts, Jardine was not quite such a bad sort as he was made out to be as a result of this unhappy episode, although I, personally, wouldn't know about that. As it happens, I only ever met him once – and that was at my Christening! He was just one of the many well-known figures of the day who were part of my mother's social set. I have no idea why he was chosen to be my Godfather and, as far as I know, I had no contact with him after he had performed his duties at the font.

As for Robert Elliott Storey Wyatt, to give him his full name, he was a lovely man, although I didn't get to know him until he was very old. We met quite by chance and, to my great mortification, I completely failed to realise exactly who he was at first.

My sister Jonet, who was living at Trelovoren in Cornwall, had invited me down to stay with her and while I was there she held a dinner party for about ten guests, all of them neighbourhood friends. As so often, I had not listened properly when the introductions were made, being too busy worrying in my usual shy way about what I was going to say to people. At the table, I found myself seated next to a very pleasant, elderly gentleman and, trying to make conversation and having quickly discovered that he was interested in sport, I launched into a monologue about my various involvements in cricket.

After yacking on for about ten minutes, I was in the middle of telling him about my batting exploits during a particular match when this white-haired old gentleman placed his hand on my arm and said quietly: "I'm so sorry to interrupt you, but your most interesting story reminds me of when I was batting with Jack Hobbs against the Australians at The Oval in 1931."

I sunk my head into my hands as the penny dropped and I suddenly realised who I must be talking to. However, he waved aside my obvious embarrassment in the most charming manner and actually seemed only too delighted to talk to someone who knew a little about the game. He very kindly invited me to lunch at his home in Truro the next day and I sat there, enthralled, as he reminisced about his 28-year playing career with Warwickshire, Worcestershire and England, including that extraordinary bodyline series in Australia. A remarkable character, he was still captaining Worcestershire at 51 and was England's oldest surviving Test player for many years until his death in 1995 at the age of 93.

Although I still blush to recall the way I had initially prattled on about my own cricketing career at my first meeting with the great man, in terms of embarrassment that incident actually pales into insignificance compared to another cricket-related occasion when, quite literally, I made a right royal fool of myself.

Tim Rice had invited me and a few other Heartaches to the Lord's Taverners Ball at the Hilton. He had a table of twelve, but a few days before the event he announced that, unfortunately, he would not actually be able to sit down with us since he had been invited to join Prince Charles at the top table.

We all totally understood the situation and assured him that we would be fine without him. The evening was going very successfully and Tim ambled over occasionally to find out how ' the peasants' were enjoying themselves. At the end of the meal, when the dancing got under way, people started table-hopping and, looking around, I spotted John Snow, the former England and Sussex bowler, whom I knew quite well, and went over to have a chat.

As we were talking, I pointed out something on the other side of the ballroom and, by chance, found myself making eye contact with Tim, who was sitting with Prince Charles and racing driver Graham

Hill. At that very moment, Prince Charles glanced in our direction and said something to Tim, who then beckoned me over. I excused myself to John, explaining that I was sorry to desert him so abruptly, but that I seemed to have received a royal summons.

I went over and, addressing Prince Charles rather nervously, said: "Good evening, Sir."

He looked up at me slightly non-plussed for a moment and then said abruptly: "I didn't ask you over. I wanted John Snow to come and have a drink."

I slunk back to my table.

I am proud to have been a member of the Lord's Taverners for many years. Accredited by the England and Wales Cricket Board as the official national charity for recreational cricket, its aim is: "To give young people, particularly those with special needs, a sporting chance"

It was founded in 1950, with HRH The Duke of Edinburgh as our Patron and Twelfth Man and Sir John Mills as our first President. Sir John's successors since then have included Jack Hawkins, Tommy Trinder, Harry Secombe, Brian Rix, Jimmy Edwards, Eric Morecombe, Ronnie Corbett, Terry Wogan, David Frost, Tim Rice, Leslie Crowther, Colin Cowdrey, Nicholas Parsons, Robert Powell – and HRH Prince Charles. We have raised millions of pounds over the years and the organisation is now divided into twenty-five regions throughout the British Isles.

Whilst working at London Weekend Television in 1986, having moved there from Capital some years before, I was invited by the late John Bromley, then head of *World of Sport* and also Chairman of the Lord's Taverners, to form a new East Sussex region. A wonderful man, who will always be sadly missed by everyone who ever worked with him, John was well aware of my connections with Rottingdean and Sussex cricket generally.

As the inaugural Chairman, my first move was to form a small committee of willing and compatible people in the area and to establish our headquarters in Brighton. Among others, the committee eventually included Eric Flackfield, a friend and recently retired Head of Presentation at LWT who lived in Brighton and was extremely well connected, Charles Dudley, an administrator at

Sussex University and Peter Earl, a self-employed accountant with many top show business names among his client list.

It happened that at around the same time I had also been asked by former Sussex county captain Peter Graves to become involved in the organisation of the first International Golden Oldies Cricket Festival to be held in this country. Sponsored by Air New Zealand, this has become a regular and hugely successful biennial event, staged in a different country each time and featuring 'friendly' 20-over matches between more than thirty teams of players aged 40+ from around the world, mostly amateurs but also including quite a few former Test stars. Real cricket jamborees, the festivals are spread over a week or ten days, with lots of social, sporting, sightseeing and cultural events in between the games, which are played at different grounds within a designated area. The first one had been staged in New Zealand in 1984 and the 1986 event was then held in Sussex, with matches all around the county. My club, Rottingdean, were to host the game between a West Indies XI and a team from New Zealand.

It occurred to me that here was great opportunity to launch the Lord's Taverners East Sussex region in style by linking it in with the International Golden Oldies event. Taking the proverbial bull by the horns, I proposed that we should book Hove Town Hall for a charity lunch for two hundred people during the Festival week. My committee agreed to give it a go, although we realised that we were up against a fairly tight time schedule, with just three weeks to organise the whole thing from scratch. Looking back, I'm amazed we even contemplated it at such short notice.

The first priority, of course, was to book the banqueting room at Hove Town Hall. I contacted the Mayor, a charming and more than helpful chap who not only confirmed that the venue was available for that date, but also offered to host a VIP reception in the Mayor's Parlour, prior to lunch.

The next task was to find some suitably interesting speakers. I got in touch with Tim Rice, a future President of the MCC and a leading Lord's Taverner and he immediately agreed. I also spoke to the wonderful Leslie Crowther, now so greatly missed, and he, too, was happy to oblige.

This was becoming tremendously exciting. All we needed to do now was to sell the two hundred tickets. But then I had another idea. I had been told that the West Indies contingent of Golden Oldies was to include Sir Gary Sobers, generally acknowledged as the greatest all-round cricketer of all time, and I wondered whether we might be able to get him along as our Guest of Honour.

Charles Dudley then told me that Gary was on the West Indies Tourist Board, obviously responsible for promoting the West Indies as a tourist attraction. Not only that, but he was a promoter of the famous Cockspur Rum. He might therefore welcome the extra publicity that his presence among us would undoubtedly bring. Charles had also found out that the West Indies Tourist Board were holding a reception at their London offices the following week at which Gary would be present and having managed to get ourselves invited through contacts at Gulliver's Travels, who were making all the travel arrangements for those taking part in the Golden Oldies Festival, we made plans to ambush him at this event with our invitation.

We duly went to the reception and waited on tenterhooks for the right moment to make our approach. And while waiting we made the most of the Tourist Board's hospitality, which included a continuous supply of Cockspur Rum cocktails, so that after an hour or so Charles and I were in a relaxed mood and ready to pounce on the great man at the first available opportunity. This eventually came when the journalists and photographers had completed their jobs and Sir Garfield was left talking to a tall and distinguished-looking silver haired West Indian gentleman. "Here we go," I muttered to Charles. "Fingers crossed!"

I moved across the room and went up to the two men, who were talking animatedly.

"Excuse me, Sir Garfield," I said. "I do hope I am not interrupting you?"

"Well, yes, as a matter of fact you are," retorted his distinguished-looking West Indian companion.

At moments like that to hesitate is fatal, so I pressed on regardless, gabbling breathlessly: "I am the Chaiman of the Lord's Taverners East Sussex Region and I have arranged a special charity lunch this Saturday for the International Golden Oldies ... and would you be our Guest of Honour?"

His distinguished-looking companion looked even more cross at my interruption, but Gary, without a moment's hesitation, smiled and said: "I would be delighted."

So, mission accomplished.

As Charles and I left, having downed yet another Cockspur Rum cocktail by way of celebration, I discovered that Gary's imposing silver-haired companion was none other than the High Commissioner of the West Indies. Had I realised that beforehand, I might not have dared to be so forthright.

Never mind. We now had the venue, a reception, two very good speakers and an illustrious Guest of Honour – but no paying customers apart from the members of our own committee. Everything hinged on doing a successful hard sell during a Happy Hour get-together in the bar at the Metropole Hotel, where the cricketers taking part in the International Golden Oldies Festival and their supporters were to be officially welcomed.

As a member of Peter Graves' IGO organising committee, I was one of the welcoming party who would be 'working the room' on that occasion. This would give me the perfect opportunity to push our Lord's Taverners lunch.

As I went around introducing myself to the various contingents from all around the globe, I came to a group of five Aussies, one of whom, a smallish chap, introduced himself as the "minder" in charge of "this unruly mob".

"I've got a coffin in my room," he drawled in a heavy Australian accent. "It's quite obvious that at least one of these bastards is going to drink himself to death before this ten-day jaunt is over, so I reckon it's best to be prepared!"

To digress for a moment, I heard the next day that a number of the Australian contingent had gone on to get themselves well inebriated around the pubs of Brighton and that one had passed out. His colleagues then took great delight in carrying him down the road and laying him out on the pavement outside the front door of a nearby funeral parlour, where he remained until he was found in the morning by people arriving for work.

Back at the Metropole, meanwhile, my new Australian friend started to introduce the other four. "This is Fred and George and Ray." We shook hands. Ray was obviously very happy, with a permanent smile, but somewhat speechless. He also looked a little familiar. I couldn't quite place him and then it suddenly hit me. I was in the company of one of the greatest bowlers of all time, the legendary Ray Lindwall.

I wasted no time in telling them about our lunch, adding that I hoped there might be an Australian table.

"Tell you what, mate," cried my new friend. "We'll not only have a table of our own, but I'll rustle up some of those bastards from New Zealand as well."

Sure enough, by the end of the evening we had filled all twenty tables.

On the morning of the lunch there were still a thousand-and-one things to do. Table plans had to be completed, waitresses briefed, menus distributed, a wine-order table arranged at the welcoming bar and the calypso band set up to play quietly in the ballroom throughout the lunch. Fortunately, everything went smoothly and the event was a huge success.

The Mayor of Hove did a marvellous job in laying on an extremely hospitable VIP reception, during which Gary Sobers made the formal presentation of a Lord's Taverners Horizon minibus to the representatives of an organisation for disadvantaged children. And among those who sat down to lunch were New Zealand stars Walter Hadlee, Bert Sutcliffe and Eric Petrie, West Indians Charlie Griffith and David Holford, Australia's Ray Lindwall, and another former Sussex captain, John Barclay.

I was in seventh heaven as I sat with Gary Sobers on my right, Walter Hadlee on my left, Tim Rice next to Gary and Leslie Crowther opposite. At regular intervals during the meal I got up to introduce the more illustrious stars, inviting the assembled company to "take wine with Gary Sobers... Ray Lindwall... Charlie Griffith..." and so on.

In his speech, Leslie Crowther then gave me a well-deserved rocket, pointing out that: "Our illustrious but stupid Chairman has been asking you to take wine with a lot of famous cricketers from countries throughout the world, but has failed to include the greatest batsman of all time after Don Bradman. So would you now stand and raise your glasses to Walter Hadlee, who, incidentally, is sitting right next to our ignorant Chairman!"

A dedicated cricket fan, Leslie was in his element and went on to have everybody in stitches. At one point he was walking around the tables with a hand-held microphone when a waitress slipped a few yards in front of him, with the result that a bread roll was sent flying out of her basket towards Leslie. He deftly caught it in his right hand and continued talking as he bowled a perfect off-break at the Australian contingent.

After the success of the lunch, I concentrated on my IGO duties and, in particular, the arrangements for the match at Rottingdean between the West Indian team, the Barbados Masters, and the Eden Park Ovalers from New Zealand. I approached the PR company that was handling Cockspur Rum and suggested they might like to dispense free samples of their product at this and other matches. This they readily agreed to do, organising a bus with banners and promotional material that travelled round from ground to ground and, not surprisingly, proved to be a very popular attraction.

I also proposed that for the Rottingdean match they should provide twenty-two Cockspur Rum cocktails for the two sides at our village pub, The Plough. This is situated close to the village pond, with the church on one side and Rudyard Kipling's house on the other. The cricket ground was a few hundred yards away. My plan was that when both teams arrived in the bus from Brighton at 11.00am they would be deposited at The Plough, where they would find the cocktails waiting for them on the bar.

During the short journey from Brighton to Rottingdean, a matter of about four miles, I took the microphone and told the players about the history of our club, getting some slightly disbelieving looks when I told them that we had played our first match in 1758.

We arrived at The Plough where all the rum cocktails were lined up on the bar. To my astonishment, the West Indian team refused to touch a drop, explaining that they did not want to consume alcohol before the match. The New Zealand lot, however, dived in and drank the whole lot in ten minutes flat.

The abstemious and very focused approach of the West Indians caused a few raised eyebrows as the whole point of the week was to promote fun and friendship. It certainly was not intended to be too fiercely competitive. The Barbados Masters, however, were clearly taking things very seriously. They were immaculately turned out with uniform blazers and grey flannels and it also emerged that while most of teams were waking up with slight hangovers, they were in the habit of starting the day with an early morning run!

I had arranged for everyone to walk from the pub to the ground so that they could enjoy to the full the environment of a beautiful English village. However, Gary Sobers was suffering from a painful knee condition, which sadly prevented him from playing, so I arranged to take him by taxi. When we arrived at the ground I suddenly realised that Gary was somewhat agitated. Having observed him taking a close interest in the racing pages of his newspaper on the bus, I suspected that his mind might be on the horses. Sure enough, just as we were getting out of the taxi he glanced round rather anxiously at the rural scene and inquired: "How does one get to put a bet on round here?"

"Easy," I replied. "You take the cab back into the village, go into The Plough and the landlord will take you round the corner to the local bookmaker."

"And how can I get some cash?" he asked.

"The landlord will cash a cheque for you," I told him.

A fair crowd was already gathering outside the ground and as Gary was about to step back inside the taxi, two elderly ladies approached with autograph books. Aware that Gary was now totally absorbed in his betting needs, I took the ladies aside and explained that he had an urgent appointment elsewhere but that he would be back shortly and would then love to sign their books. A look of sheer desperation came into their eyes, so I assured them: "Please don't worry, he really will be back in twenty minutes."

"Do you promise?" they pleaded, adding, much to my amazement: "We've come all the way from Aberdeen just to meet him."

The match itself took an unexpected course. As I have already explained, the whole idea was to hold a festival of cricket where the results were of little consequence compared to the camaraderie and overall enjoyment of a week's international gathering. The Barbados Masters, however, made it clear that they were not just there for the beer – or even the Cockspur rum cocktails! The matches were restricted to twenty overs per team, so one could normally expect the average score to be around 180, but the Masters went out and thrashed the bowling all round the ground, amassing an unbelievable total of 297-2.

The Ovallers staggered in for lunch looking slightly shell-shocked and totally exhausted after repeatedly chasing the ball to the boundary, but their attitude was brilliant. When I asked them if they were all right they responded with cheery grins and said it was privilege to be playing against such famous cricketers of the past. As their team also featured several veteran ex-Test players I thought that was quite a compliment.

Accompanying the Masters, although not actually playing, was the fearsome former West Indian fast bowler Charlie Griffith. The team had actually brought more followers than expected so we ran out of chicken salad and had to provide quiche instead. Charlie, a giant of a man, gazed with obvious distaste at this offering and growled: "I ain't eating this muck." Whereupon the team's minder, a very large West Indian lady with an enormous bosom, bellowed: "Shut up and eat the f****** quiche, Charlie!" He shot her a terrified glance and reverted into cuddly lamb mode.

His colleagues duly bowled the Ovallers out for 88, but the New Zealanders accepted defeat with a very good grace and retired to the bar to drown their sorrows, while the Masters went on to dish out even greater punishment in a later match, scoring a record 353-7 and then reducing the opposition to 22-5 before rain mercifully stopped play. What had been another wonderful day for me ended with drinks back at the Metropole with a group that included Gary Sobers and Ray Lindwall.

Magic!

Three days later my telephone rang at 7.00am and a cheery voice said: "Hello, Gary here." I had a colleague at LWT called Gary Knight and I assumed it must be him. As usual, I had not got to bed until around 2.00am, so I was not best pleased by this rude awakening. "What the bloody hell do you think you're doing, Gary, phoning me at this ungodly hour?" Unfortunately, it was not Gary from work – it was Gary Sobers.

Now, swearing at a god is not usually a sensible thing to do, but Gary seemed to take it very calmly. All he wanted to know was how to get up to London as he had lost his minder for a few days. I happily arranged a taxi, went with it to pick him up, took him to the station, got his ticket and put him on the train As we were saying goodbye, I nervously said: "How about lunch in London some time?"

To my amazement, he said he would be delighted and would ring me after he returned from a trip to Canada that he was about to undertake. And, true to his word, he did just that. Three months later he rang to remind me of my invitation. Quite apart from the wonderful prospect of lunching with the man who, along with Don Bradman and Denis Compton, was one of my greatest heroes, I have to admit that I was keen to make sure that I took him somewhere where his presence as my guest would attract the most kudos. So, where to go?

I quickly discounted Indian, Chinese or Italian, toyed briefly with the idea of somewhere posh like The Savoy Grill or the Dorchester and then realised that for maximum impact there was really only one place to be seen – the LWT restaurant.

For years my colleagues at work had been accusing me of serial name-dropping through my involvement with the Lord's Taverners. This was the moment to prove once and for all that it wasn't just so much hot air. I booked my table and prayed that as many as possible of my friends would choose to eat in the restaurant that day rather than going out.

My prayers were answered. There was a full house. And as I walked in with Sir Gary, the astonished silence that fell over certain tables, accompanied by dropping jaws, gave me the most tremendous satisfaction. I was a very happy bunny.

That wasn't the only bit of cricketing one-upmanship I enjoyed during that glorious and eventful summer. As President of Rottingdean, I decided that it would be fun to arrange an 18th-century match to be played as it would have been in 1758, when the club recorded its first match.

The village fair at Rottingdean is always held on the first Saturday in August and each year it has a different theme, with everybody in the village getting involved. In the seventies and eighties the event, not to say the whole village, was run by Mrs Betty Dacre, a formidable lady whose father had founded St Dunstan's, which was originally intended for servicemen blinded during the Great War and was located just a mile from Rottingdean. An incredible personality, held in awe by all who came into her orbit, Mrs Dacre had very strong opinions on how the village should be run and no one dared to offer alternatives.

I nevertheless plucked up the courage to suggest that if she were to opt for an 18th-century theme, all the stallholders could dress up in the costume of the period while the cricket club could recreate the match of 1758 with not only the sporting attire but also the bats and stumps of that period. Mrs Dacre thought this was a great idea and, of course, everyone on her committee agreed. I also spoke to the wonderful Leslie Crowther, and he, too, was happy to oblige.

Maurice Angel, the renowned theatrical costumier in Tottenham Court Road did a roaring trade in 18th-century cricket apparel, including cocked hats, frock coats and breeches and, on the day, it all went brilliantly. Leslie, as always, was a star. The weather held and the 18th-century parade through the village was a triumph.

The cricket match was also a huge success and *The Cricketer* – now *The Wisden Cricketer* – a monthly magazine with a circulation of over 40,000, ran an eye-catching cover photograph of me tossing up with the two captains.

What's more, I achieved immortality in the eyes of the whole village when I was heard by all and sundry to address Mrs Dacre as 'Betty' – something no one had ever dared to do before.

# XI
## A GOOD INNINGS

THE RESTAURANT at London Weekend Television was open to all two thousand members of the staff, but it was certainly a cut above your average company canteen. The food was excellent, there was a decent wine list and, being subsidised by the company, it was very reasonably priced. In fact, the only inhibiting factor to some staff was the possibility that they could find themselves sitting at the next table to the Managing Director or other members of the Board.

As far as the Advertising Sales Department was concerned, it was a particularly good place to entertain clients, as they were quite likely to find themselves rubbing shoulders with stars of stage and screen, which always went down well.

On one occasion, four of us were enjoying a good lunch with a few bottles of wine when a tiny, one-eyed, coloured chap wandered over from his table and squatted down before us, holding a glass of brandy. "Hi, chaps - howya doin?" he inquired. It was Sammy Davis Jr.

Service in the restaurant was provided by three extremely extroverted, middle-aged waitresses headed by May, a very outspoken Irish woman with a great sense of humour and occasion. I decided one day to invite my Trustee to lunch. He was eighty years old by this time and the sort of man who would have been more at home in the National Liberal Club. I was aware, however, that he had an eye for attractive women and that he was sure to enjoy a few 'sightings' of celebrities.

It was very important for me that the lunch went well because this gentleman controlled my grandfather's Trust, through which I continued to derive an enjoyable private income. I therefore decided that it would be as well to brief May in advance so as to avoid any possible embarrassment. "I'm lunching with an important gentleman tomorrow, May," I explained. "I need to impress him because he has control of my financial future, so could you please, for once, show some respect? For instance, I'd prefer it if you didn't call me 'Tony'. Perhaps, when we come in, you could say something like: 'Good morning, Sir. How nice to see you. I hope you and Mr Salisbury enjoy your lunch.' Have you got that, May?"

"Certainly Tony," she said. "You can rely on me. No problem."

The next day I entered the restaurant with the venerable old gentleman. "Good morning, Sir. Good morning Mr. Salisbury," said May. "I hope you have an enjoyable lunch. And may I bring you a wine list, Mr Salisbury, so that you can make a selection at your convenience?"

There was a moment's pause and then May, with a despairing sigh, dug me in the ribs and said: "Oi! Tony, mate. How long have I got to go on keeping up this bloody lark?"

My Trustee, of course, loved it. May, as usual, had read the situation perfectly.

After three eventful years at Capital, I had returned to my roots in television with LWT in 1976. And I have to say that I felt much more at home there. Life at Capital had been quite stressful at times, especially when the station was going through a rather rocky financial period.

I was with LWT for eleven years, right up until my retirement in 1987 at the age of sixty. This was a sad moment for me, but I'm proud to say that my colleagues saw me out in style.

The Advertising Sales Department had a reputation for knowing how to lay on a bit of a knees-up. Take Gary's stag night, for instance.

Gary was one of our sales managers, a Cockney with a huge head of curly hair, very popular with everyone.

A colleague took on the arrangements for the day's activities, which were pretty formidable and somewhat complicated, but only on a par with the standards expected of the department's social activities.

There were twenty-five of us involved and the agenda took in five locations throughout the day and night. As the plans unfolded, I was seriously worried that I would not be able to sustain the pace. I was twenty years older than my colleagues and my capacity and stamina were beginning to lessen.

The first stop was to be The Antelope, one of my 'locals' since the 1950s when it was also frequented by the likes of Heath and Haig – both hanged for horrific murders – Jimmy Goldsmith, John Aspinall and many other interesting and colourful characters.

We all met up there at about 11.00am on a Saturday morning and beer, wine, champagne and whatever else was requested flowed until we were due to leave for lunch at 2.30pm. A French-style open-deck bus had been hired for the day. The back of the bus had a platform that accommodated two barrels of beer, which we consumed on our way to the restaurant in Piccadilly.

For some reason the organisers, who shall remain nameless but were led by Michael Lench, had booked a table in this establishment without first 'sussing' its attitude towards the flexibility of opening hours, especially with regard to the licensing laws, and its tolerance of the sort of behaviour to be expected from lively television executives out on the razzle.

We arrived at 2.50pm and sat ourselves around one large table. Up until this point everything had been going very smoothly, but now came the first hiccup.

The waitress announced that in ten minutes no more orders for food or drink could be taken and so could we please make up our minds quickly.

That did not test the brain cells too sharply and after a quick mental calculation someone called out: "Twenty-five bottles of dry white, twelve bottles of house red, three bottles of Courvoisier and two bottles of port, please. Oh! And twenty-five omelettes."

The waitress departed, giggling, and within minutes returned with a couple of colleagues and placed all the booze on the table.

"Omelettes are on the way" she said. "And all drinks must be consumed by 3.00pm." She then left. We put most of the drink under the table and the party progressed. As we finished eating, we noticed that preparations were being made for another party in the balcony area above us. It turned out to be a children's party, complete with a magician. There were twenty or thirty children with their mothers and a magician in a top hat.

The manager of the restaurant was beginning to get a bit stroppy with us by this time, indicating that all kinds of licensing laws were being broken and suggesting fairly forcefully that we should settle the enormous bill and depart. In the middle of this there was, for no apparent reason, a moment of complete silence, broken by the sound of the magician saying: "And now, children, what do you think I've got in this top hat?"

It was temptation beyond endurance. I would defy anyone with a normal, dirty mind to come up with any lewd suggestion that was not shouted out by the wits among our group.

Pandemonium ensued. Mothers cried and clapped hands over their children's ears. The magician started hurling abuse at us. The manager stood rooted to the spot not knowing which way to turn. To use that term beloved of *News of the World* journalists, we made our excuses and left. Hurriedly.

The plan was to move on to another drinking club before going to the East End for the evening. Realising that my stamina was unlikely to hold up for the whole day and night, I opted to take a breather at this stage and went home, promising to rejoin everyone at 7pm in a certain East End public house.

Back at home, I had a kip and then took a bath and changed in readiness for the next round. Knowing that our last stop was to be in another well-known East End pub where we were to be 'entertained', having a fair idea of what this 'entertainment' would involve and suspecting that, as the oldest member of the group, I might be selected for some 'special' treatment, I decided to put on my cricket 'box', just in case.

The pub was crowded with regulars when we all stumbled in at 11.00pm. It was very noisy, with extremely loud music and a great atmosphere. To someone like me, who had never before ventured deep into the East End so late at night, it was all rather unnerving.

The landlord, who could best be described as West Ham's answer to Bernard Manning, rang a large bell at 11.30pm and bellowed: "A private party is about to start now, so the rest of your can sod off!"

The regulars, who seemed used to this sort of thing, departed noisily. We then settled ourselves at various tables around the bar and the landlord went into his welcoming act. It was brilliant – or, at least, it seemed so with the booze we had consumed – but I would not have taken my Aunt Dora along.

After his performance, he introduced two blondes, who, without any preamble, took off all their clothes and started writhing around on the carpet. This went on for about ten minutes and then they got up and began gyrating in front of us. My apprehensions about the course the evening's entertainment might take were then proved absolutely correct. One of the blondes, who had been eyeing me up and down whilst wriggling around, suddenly came over and plonked herself on my lap. Now, I've certainly never taken off all my clothes and sat on the lap of a colleague wearing a box and it was quite obvious from this young lady's reaction that, although she had been around a bit in her professional life, this was a unique experience for her, too.

You could almost hear her mind working. This was either the most exciting and original 'thing' she had sat on in her life or the most horribly deformed object ever created. She decided it must be the latter and, with a shrill scream, jumped off and reverted to gyrating elsewhere. An interval was then announced and I knew I was now safe from any further 'interference'.

However, for reasons that I can't quite explain, but which must have had something to do with the amount of alcohol I had consumed and a desire to show off, I let it drop to the landlord that I had been to Eton and also that I had been a Cavalry Officer. This was a particularly stupid thing to do in the depths of the East End. Grabbing the microphone to conclude the evening's entertainment with another bout of his stand-up 'comedy', he proceeded to take the mickey out of me in a devastating manner. I began to think it would have been less embarrassing to let the stripper have her evil way with me!

Recalling this particular shindig, I was a little apprehensive as my retirement approached, wondering what surprises my colleagues might have in store for me. In fact, I needn't have worried – they did me proud, but let me off lightly.

There were several little farewell dos, culminating in a dinner party organised by our Sales Director, Ron Miller, in the Executive Suite at Kent House, now the South Bank Television Centre. All my best mates over the years were invited.

Unbeknownst to me, Ron had arranged that instead of dinner jackets, cricket gear should be the order of the day. Everyone duly obliged, including my old friend Graham Dowson, who was about to become my business partner in a marketing consultancy venture. Large but perfectly formed, the sight of Graham leaving his Barbican flat in full cricket whites, including a little cap perched on top of his head, must have astounded the doormen and porters.

Other friends present included Tony Vickers, who had been with me at Capital as Sales Director and had gone on to do the same job at the revived TV-AM, Harry Theobalds, the recently retired Head of Advertising Control at the Independent Broadcasting Authority who had also gone to TV-AM, and John Fox, who had been with me at Southern Television before moving on to Television South. It was a great evening that lasted long into the night – and to top it all, Ron presented me with two plane tickets to Sydney to see the Australia v. England Test Match that autumn.

In view of all this generosity, I decided to host a dinner for the LWT Advertising Sales department on the evening of my departure. My favourite eating hole at the time was the Sambuca, an upmarket Italian restaurant in Symonds Street, just off Sloane Square. This was where Jeffrey Archer was famously supposed to have had a vital dinner engagement, only to get his comeuppance when he was found to have lied about the date.

The headwaiter there was Valerio, whom Jill and I had known ever since the Sambuca first opened years before. He now runs Scalini in Walton Street, which is every bit as good as the Sambuca, if not better, and is now my favourite restaurant. As with Sambuca, its success is due almost entirely to Valerio's personality. He is on duty six days a week for lunch and dinner. The place is always packed, usually with a sprinkling of top sportsmen. At various times, I have found myself sitting next to Brian Lara, David Gower, Richie

Benaud, Terry Venables, Don King – and even 'Fergie', the Duchess of York.

Back at Sambuca, I sat down with the owner, Sandro, and asked if I could book the whole place for sixty guests. He kindly agreed and we discussed the cost. I explained that I wanted a small area at the end of the restaurant cleared of tables so that I could welcome my guests for pre-dinner drinks. I wanted three courses and selected them from his menu. We then discussed the drink requirements. Sandro said that he usually worked on the basis that each guest would have a gin-and-tonic or a beer on arrival, an average of half a bottle of wine with dinner and a liqueur with coffee.

"I think that could prove a little on the conservative side for this lot," I said. "You should be prepared for around three large gin and tonics or whiskies per head before dinner and at least a bottle-and-a-half of wine each with the meal. And when it comes to the coffee and liqueurs, we will require a bottle of Courvoisier between two."

For once in his life this normally voluble and excitable Italian restaurateur was silent. In fact, his mouth was agape.

"But Tony," he eventually responded. "I thought you said there would be women present."

"There certainly will be," I said. "But if you think that a woman sales executive at London Weekend Television has any lesser social requirements than the blokes, you would not only be seriously wrong. You would also be insulting their stamina and ability."

We eventually agreed an overall sum, based on my brief.

The plan was that I would pay half while my colleagues paid the rest at so much per head. What I did not know was that, even as I was making my own preparations, a series of secret meetings were taking place in the office at which various embellishments were being planned.

Firstly, they arranged for Rolf Harris's pianist to play certain tunes at a piano that was smuggled in a few hours before the start of the evening. These tunes included such familiar melodies as Gilbert & Sullivan's 'Tit Willow, Tit Willow', but with the lyrics rewritten and circulated on song sheets to everyone in advance. The resulting ditties, mostly composed under the direction of Tony Darrell-Brown, were rendered by the entire ensemble at the end of the meal, before the arrival of the coffee and liqueurs. Some were rude and some not so rude, but they were all about me and I actually found them downright moving. I can't read them today without my eyes misting over.

As if that wasn't enough, Adrian Tracey, another very great friend, suddenly appeared with a large wrapped offering. It was a portrait of me in cricket clothes at Rottingdean, which they had had painted from a photograph.

To say that all this was too much for me would be an understatement.

The evening finished at around 4.00am the next morning. And at midday I returned to settle my account.

Sandro sat down with an awed expression on his face.

"I have been in the restaurant business all my life," he said. "In fact, I started with Mario & Franco. And yet I have never, ever seen so much drink consumed by so few people over such a long period – and some of them were women! But I have to say that apart from everyone being exceedingly exuberant, no-one behaved badly or did anything to upset residents nearby. It's unbelievable."

"Well, Sandro," I said. "That's LWT for you. Now, what's the damage?"

Sandro mentioned a figure 50% higher than we had agreed.

"Now, come on Sandro," I said. "We agreed on …"

"OK, OK," he sighed, raising his hands in resignation. He was part Moroccan, as well as an Italian.

At sixty, I wasn't ready to retire completely. In fact, after thirty years my career in broadcasting now came full circle when I got together with my great friend Graham Dowson to form a marketing consultancy, Dowson Salisbury, that was to provide a happy final chapter to the story of my working life.

One way and another, it's been a pretty good innings. If I had to name one regret I suppose it would be that I never married, thus missing out on family life. On the other hand, I would have to admit that the bachelor lifestyle has always suited me rather well. And although I have no children of my own, I do have countless nephews and nieces who have now made me a great-uncle several times over.

I am especially fond of Tatiana, Jonet's daughter by her first husband, Ivan Kennedy. Tatiana – or 'Tats', as she is affectionately known – has always been a free spirit and a wonderfully strong character without whose encouragement this book would probably never have been written.

Ivan's father was a White Russian – hence the name Tatiana – and, while Ivan himself was a wonderfully extrovert character, his mother, Sonia, was even more colourful, a complete one-off. She spoke English with a wonderfully fractured accent, had very strong and often outrageous views about everything and also 'read' the cards. Soon after I met her for the first time, I happened to be visiting her at her home in Bywater Street, Chelsea one day when she announced: "Anthony, I read your fortune".

She took a pack of cards and started turning them over one by one. Suddenly the black Queen of Spades was turned up. With a cry of alarm, Sonia gathered the cards and threw them into a drawer, shouting: "I tell no more cards!" She refused to say what had spooked her, which made it all the more unnerving. I was about twenty-five at the time and spent the next few years waiting anxiously for the black queen to strike!

On another occasion, I spent Christmas Day with Ivan, Jonet, Tatiana and Sonia. Ivan was tremendous company and a great host who enjoyed the social life with a vengeance. During the morning we all partook of the usual festive hospitality, while Sonia remained in the kitchen, attending not only to the turkey, but also to the Christmas pudding – and paying special attention to the preparation of the brandy butter. By the time she'd finished tasting it, to make sure that the alcoholic content was just right, she had devoured virtually the whole lot. As a result she was decidedly shaky on her feet by the time lunch was ready and had to be taken upstairs and put to bed.

After lunch we decided to go for a walk and, thinking that Sonia would have slept it off by this time and would be able to join us, shouted to her to come down. She appeared rather unsteadily at the top of the stairs, looked down at us, leant forward and, as if in slow motion, toppled down the twenty odd stairs.

We all gathered round this crumpled lady, enormously concerned. Complete silence reigned. Then, looking up at our anxious faces she fixed Ivan with an accusing look and said in a very strong, loud voice: "Son, you pushed me!"

We put her to bed again and went for our walk.

Tatiana is married to Hilary Tunstall-Behrens who, amongst other things, stages classical music concerts at Trelovoren, the 12th-century house near Truro that has been his family's home for generations. The couple's wedding took place in the private chapel there and I was asked to say a few words at the reception afterwards.

Although I normally hate having to speak at any big occasions, I was not too worried in Tatiana's case as I knew – or thought I knew – that her guests would be friendly, were likely to appreciate my efforts and might even manage to laugh at my weak jokes.

I proceeded to rough out a speech, containing all the usual rather rude, hackneyed jokes and sentimental platitudes. Big mistake! What I hadn't fully appreciated was that Hilary being a dedicated classical music buff who had arranged musical festivals not only at Trelovoren but throughout Cornwall, the majority of the guests he had invited shared this interest. They even included a couple of well-known music critics. My personal musical tastes being a little less highbrow – jazz, rock'n'roll and Frank Sinatra are more my style – I was not exactly in my element and it dawned on me that my speech was unlikely to strike a chord, as it were.

I did not become aware of this until the morning of the wedding, so I was well and truly stuffed, not to say panic-stricken. The wedding went well and everybody gathered for the breakfast. I was seated at the top table and found myself gazing at this throng of young, earnest classical music enthusiasts with mounting apprehension. Knowing that my prepared speech was likely to go down like the proverbial lead balloon, I frantically tried to think of ways to adlib.

I happened to overhear that one of the guests was a young man called Steven Isserlis and that he was regarded as the country's second leading cellist after Julian Lloyd-Webber. I seized on this as an excuse to make what I thought would be a funny remark that would surely be received hilariously and would show everybody how knowledgeable I was about the classical music scene.

My idea was to make an opening quip referring to Mr Isserlis and welcoming him to the feast in the manner of someone reading the football results on television, something along the lines of: "Julian Lloyd Webber 1, Steven Isserlis 2". I could imagine this bringing the house down and I grew more relaxed as the time for me to speak drew nearer. The only slight problem was that having never heard of Steven up until that day, I wasn't entirely sure about how to pronounce his surname.

Sitting next to me was one my sister's closest friends who not only shared my mother's real name of Muriel, but who also happened to be her very double – tall, thin and outspoken, with a wicked sense of humour. As I was preparing to get up and speak I consulted her about the correct pronunciation. She waited until I had risen to my feet and then tugged my sleeve, looked up at me and hissed: "It rhymes with syphilis!"

In an instant, I sensed my balloon turning to lead once again.

I thought it would be appropriate to end this tome with a little cricketing story:

It was my first – and only – league match at, and for, Streatham, where I was playing as a guest of the skipper, my great friend Peter Beecheno, sadly no longer with us. (Incidentally, Peter's wife, Anita, who is Dutch and nicknamed 'Curly', is a former captain of both the Dutch Women's national cricket side and also the national hockey team.)

Anyway, I went in to bat and a few balls later stroked the ball to extra cover – an easy two runs. As I trotted back to complete the second, I saw that extra cover had thrown the ball high to the wicket keeper and that it was going to descend straight into his waiting hands, over the stumps.

As I got to within a foot of the crease I realised that if I were to proceed any further the wicket keeper would become momentarily unsighted and that the ball might hit him on the nut! So, concerned for his safety, I stopped inches short of the crease and raised my bat and my other arm above my head, so that he would have clear view of the ball.

The following then happened:

The ball dropped into the keeper's hands.

I said: "All right, mate?"

He answered 'Yep', at the same time whipping off the bails and adding: "Howzat?"

The umpire nodded sympathetically and told me: "Sorry, chum, you have to go."

The keeper shrugged and said: "It's your own bloody fault – you're in the league now, you know!"

I strode off without any show of dissent in the face of what I regarded as distinctly unsportsmanlike behaviour, not at all in the spirit of the game that I had grown up with. My only comment as I headed back towards the pavilion was: "Well, at least this chap's got a code."

ACCT 144, 147
Adams, Paul 44
Adcock, Trevor 80-1
Advertising Magazines 93
Air New Zealand 157
Alberta 62-3
Aldwyn, Earl St 107
Anderson, James 133
Andes, the SS 101, 102-3
Antelope, The 44, 46, 97, 112, 169
Archer, Fred 56-7
Archer, Jeffrey 172
Ard Na Sidhe 107
Ark Royal 77
Armoured Brigade, 2nd 29
Armstrong, Louis 117
Ascot, Royal 40
Ash, Jeremy 25-6
Aspel, Michael 153
Aspinall, John 169
Astor, The 119
Astoria, The 55
Attenborough, Lord 'Dickie' 132, 137, 138, 139, 141-3
ATV 94
Aylestone, Lord 136-7


Bagatelle, The 44
Banff 62
Bankhead, Tallulah 11, 12
Baker, Tom 126
Barbados Masters 161, 162, 163
Barclay, Alex 10, 11, 13, 23, 28-9
Barclay, John 160
Barnes, Jan 7, 41, 42
Bassey 11
Beacon Hill 67, 69
Beck, Jack 127
Beecheno, Peter 80, 81-2, 177
Beecheno, Anita 177
Bell-Syre, Bill 44-5
Benaud, Richie 173
Beria, Prince 108
Berkeley Grill, The 44

Blanchflower, Danny 135
Blyth, Henry 70
Boat Race, the 48
Bovingdon Camp 23-4
Bradman, Don 9, 153-4, 161, 164
Brettenham House 85, 87
Brighton 67, 76, 77, 156, 159, 161
Brighton Belle 72, 118
Brighton Brunswick 74
Brighton Pier 77
British Columbia 62-3
Brittain, RSM 24-5
Brittenden, Arthur 7, 89-91
'Broadcast' 141
Bromley, John 156
Bubba 11, 12
Bukht, Michael 141
Bunch of Grapes, The 118


Calgary 62, 65
Camel Legion, Arab 42
Canada 57, 61, 72
Canberra, the SS 105
Cannes 109
Canterbury, Archbishop of 92-3
Capital Radio 132, 135, 137-148, 149, 156, 168 172
Carlton Tower Hotel 118, 131
Carousel, The 140
Cavendish Hotel 30-1
Cecil, Lord Hugh 18
Chamberlain, Neville 14
Chapman, Eddie 46
Charles, Prince 155
Chirk Castle 13
Churchill, Winston 102
Coates, 'Pop' 70, 71
Cockspur Rum 158, 159, 161, 163
Compton, Denis 164
Corbett, Ronnie 156
Covington, Julie 150
Coward, Noel 102
Cowdrey, Colin 156
'Cricketer, The' 165

Crosby, Bing 48
Crowther, Leslie 153, 156, 157, 160-1, 165
Cuckfield 79

Dacre, Betty 165
*Daily Mail, The* 89
Danielli Hotel 30
Darrell-Brown, Tony 7, 173
Davies, Dickie 94
Davies, Jack 70
Davis, Sammy Jnr 167
D'eath, Clarence 95-6
D'eath, Robin 133
'Deep Throat' 147
Derby, The 40
Dexter, Ted 120, 153
de Walden, Lord and Lady Howard 13, 40
Ditchling 79
'Dixon of Dock Green' 130
Dorchester, The 97, 98, 164
'Double Your Money' 95
Dowson, Denise 7
Dowson, Graham 7, 95-8, 101-3, 116, 172, 174
Dowson Salisbury 174
Dudley, Charles 7, 156-7, 158

Earl, Peter 156-7
Eden Park Ovalers 161, 163
Edinburgh, Duke of 156
Edmonton 62-3
Edmundsbury 10, 11, 18
Edrich, John 126
Edward VII, King 30-1
Edwards, Jimmy 156
Egypt 32, 36
El Alamein 29
Ellern, Hans 72-3
Ellern Paper Company 72
Empress of England, the SS 101, 103

England & Wales Cricket Board 156
Eton 13, 14-15, 18-20, 23, 40, 70, 146, 171
*Evening Standard*, the 73, 139
'Evita' 150

Fairbanks, Douglas Snr 102
Fairbanks, Douglas Jnr 11
Ffrench-Blake, Neil 130, 132, 136
Findon 79
Flackfield, Eric 156
Fletcher, Robin 141
Flynn, Erroll 119
'Food & Drink' 141
Fookes, Janet MP 132
Forbes, Brian 132
Forsyth, Bruce 135
Fox, John 7, 172
France, the SS 104
Friends of Rottingdean, the 153
Frost, David 156

Gallant Squire 115-16
'Ghandi' 142
Gliddon, Mike 129
Gloucester, Duke of 11, 13
Gloucester, Duchess of 13
Goldsmith, Jimmy 169
Gorst, John MP 139
Goss, Jack 121, 124
Gould, Jimmy 80
Gower, David 173
Grade, Lord Lew 94
Graham, Archie 90, 92-3
Graveney, Tom 151
Graves, Peter 157, 159
Greene, Hughie 95
Griffin, John 30
Griffith, Charlie 160, 163
Great Universal Stores (GUS) 10, 39, 53, 55
Gulliver's Travels 158

Hadlee, Walter 160, 161
Hammond, Wally 9
Hanley, Jimmy 93
Hargreaves, Allan 146
Harker, Gordon 27
Harris, Rolf 173
Hawkins, Jack 156
Harrods 41
Harrow 15, 40
Harry's Bar 30
Head of the River Race 49
Heartaches, the 149-152, 155
Henfield 77, 79-80
Henley 40
Hereford Arms, the 44, 51
Hess, Myra 48
Hill, Graham 155-6
Hobbs, Jack 155
Hobley, McDonald 126
Holford, David 160
Hove, Mayor of 157, 160
Howard, Leslie 11
Hulbert, Jack 118
Hunt, Marsha 145-6
Hurst, Geoff 127
Hussars, 10th 28
Hussein, King of Jordan 25

Independent Broadcasting Authority
  (IBA) 129, 130, 132, 134, 135, 136, 137,
  138, 139, 140, 144, 146
Independent Television Authority
  (ITA) 90
International Golden Oldies 157-163
Isserlis, Steven 176-7

Jaranda, the 44, 47, 51
Jacobs, David 132
Jagger, Mick 145
Jardine, Douglas 15, 154
Jones, Buck 115

Kennedy, Ivan 175
Kennedy, Paddy 45
King, Don 173
Kipling, Rudyard 120, 161
Knight, Gary 163-4
Knightsbridge Casino 136
Krupa, Gene 117
Kyle, Raymond 7

Lagonda Coupe 71
Lara, Brian 173
Larwood, Harold 154
LBC 132, 140
Leander Rowing Club 49
Lee, Peggy 117
Lenham, Les 120
Lench, Michael 169
Lewes 70
Lewis, Rosa 30-32
Lindwall, Ray 160, 163
Litchfield, Lord 145
Lloyd George, David MP 10
Lloyd-Webber, Andrew 150
Lloyd-Webber, Julian 176
Local Radio Association 139
Lollobrigida, Gina 146
*London Evening News* 72
London Weekend Television (LWT)
  156, 164, 167, 168, 172, 173, 174
Longford, Lord 146-7
Lonsdale, Norman 26-28
Lord's 15, 53
Lord's Taverners 7, 17, 155, 164
  East Sussex Region 156-61

Madeira 101-4, 106
Manning, Bernard 171
Marlar, Robin 153
Marmor, Robin 133
Marseille 109
Martin, Biddy 111-12
Martin, George 132

Marvin, Lee 118
Mason, 35-6
Maugham, Somerset 102
MCC 157
Miell, John 88, 97-8
Milburn, Colin 124
Miles, Michael 95-6
Miller, Maureen 7
Miller, Ron 7, 172
Mills, Sir John 156
Milroy, The 44
Mitchelson, Sir Archie 9, 10-11, 38, 43, 107
Monte Carlo 108
Montreal 58
Morecambe, Eric 126, 156
Mountbatten, Lord Louis and Lady Edwina 11, 13
'Mrs Dale's Diary' 130
Myers, Liza 7, 147

Napoleon 119-20
NATKE 147
Neagle, Dame Anna 142
Newhaven 81
Nielsen A.C. 96, 116
Northumberland, Duke of 15
NUJ 147

Oakman, Alan 120
O'Brien, Vincent 107, 114
O'Callaghan, Larry 113
Odeon, Leicester Square 56
Officer Cadet Training Unit 23-4, 28, 29, 42
Olivier, Sir Lawrence 118
Orchid Room, The 44
Oughton, Alan 114-15

Palmanova 29, 32, 34
Palm Beach Casino 113
Parkinson, Michael 126

Parks, Jim 120-3
Parsons, Nicholas 156
Pasha, Glubb 42
Penney, John 30
Pentagram 143
Peters, Sylvia 132
Petrie, Eric 160
Pettifer, Julian 94-5
Philip, Prince 44
Pigalle, The 88
Plough, The 82, 120, 123, 161, 162
Plumpton 114
Pontin, Fred 17-18
Port Said 34, 36
Pountain, Bob 124-6
Powell, Robert 156
Pratt, Mr 43-4
Price, Ryan 114
Priday, Edward 7
Procter & Gamble 85, 88-9, 92

Quaglinos 44
Queen, HM The 92-3
Queen's Bays 14, 23, 28, 29
Queen Mother, HM The 115

Radio 1 129
Rank Organisation 55, 97, 101
Raven, Simon 145
Reading 75-6
Reading Ladies Bowling Club 75
Reid's Hotel 102
Rice, Sir Tim 7, 149-51, 155, 160
Rix, Brian 156
Rocky Mountains 62
Roddick, Mark 28-9, 107-8, 114
Roffey 79
Ros, Edmundo 44
Rottingdean 52, 70, 118, 127, 161, 165
Rottingdean Cricket Club 67-72, 77, 79-80, 120, 153-4, 156, 157, 164-5, 174
Royal Albert Hall 48

Salisbury Family
  Jack (father) 10, 31, 146
  Muriel (mother) 9, 12, 42, 60, 70,
    107-9, 154
  Jonet (sister) 7, 11, 12, 42-3, 44, 71,
    154, 174, 175
  Amanda (sister) 7, 11, 116
  Tatiana (niece) 174-6
Sambuca 172
Sapper, Alan 144
Savoy, The 85, 93, 164
Scaynes Hill 79
Searle, 24
Secombe, Harry 156
Sergeant, Johnny 7
Sergeant, Tim 7
Sharpe, Lady 137
Sheridan, Dinah 93
Sherrin, Ned 132, 136
Sinatra, Frank 176
Smith, C. Aubrey 80
Smith, Don 120
Smith, Prof Tony 132, 133, 136
Snow, John 122-3, 155-6
Sobers, Sir Garfield (Gary) 157-9,
    160, 162, 163-4
Southern Television 72, 73, 85, 111,
    112, 116, 129, 133
Speldhurst 147
St. Aubyn's 70, 71, 127
St. James 81
Star Tavern 44, 45-7
Stirling, Colonel 132
Stockwood, Mervyn 135
Sutcliffe, Bert 160
Suttle, Ken 120

'Take Your Pick' 95
'The Clouds Are High' 81
'The Domestic Cricketer' 81
Theobalds, Harry 172
Thompson, John 137
Tito 29
Tracey, Adrian 7, 174

Trelovoren 154, 176
Trieste 29, 30, 34
Trinder, Tommy 156
Tunstall-Behrens, Hilary 176
TV-AM 172

Unilever 85, 92
Union Castle 129

Valerio 7, 172
Vancouver 58, 59, 62
Venables, Terry 173
Venice 30, 32, 34
Vickers, Tony 141, 172
Vogt, John 129

Walton Street 41-3, 44, 51, 70
Waugh, Evelyn 31
Webb, Rupert 120
Webber, Eric 70, 71, 72, 77
Webber, Barbie 70, 71, 72
Webber, Stephanie 72
Webber, Toni 72
Wellington, the Duke of 44, 46
Wells, Paddy 42
West Indies Tourist Board 158
Whitney, John 139
Who, Dr 126
Wilding, Jo 139
Willis, Lord Ted 130, 132, 135, 136-9
Wilson, Norman 74, 76
Wilson, Roddy 42
Wisdom, Norman 70
Wise, Ernie 126
Wogan, Terry 156
World Cup 126-7
Woolfson, Isaac 10
Wyatt, R.E.S (Bob) 153, 154-5
Wynn, Greville 91, 92

York, Duchess of 173